Software as a Service Inflection Point

Using Cloud Computing to Achieve Business Agility

Melvin B. Greer, Jr

iUniverse, Inc.
New York   Bloomington

Software as a Service Inflection Point
Using Cloud Computing to Achieve Business Agility

iUniverse books may be ordered through booksellers or by contacting:

iUniverse
1663 Liberty Drive
Bloomington, IN 47403
www.iuniverse.com
1-800-Authors (1-800-288-4677)

ISBN: 978-1-4401-4196-6 (pbk)
ISBN: 978-1-4401-4195-9 (hc)
ISBN: 978-1-4401-4197-3 (ebk)

Printed in the United States of America

iUniverse rev. date: 4/27/2009

Critical acclaim for Melvin Greer's

Software as a Service Inflection Point

Using Cloud Computing to Achieve Business Agility

"True to form, Melvin Greer's futurist thinking provides new applicability to Software as a Service that identifies ways of reducing costs, creating greater efficiencies, and ultimately providing significant long-term value through business transformation. He continues to be on the cutting edge of merging business function evolution and technology innovation to increase customer satisfaction and return on investments."

Kevin Manuel-Scott
Chairman and CEO
RONIN IT Services, LLC

"Melvin Greer provides an excellent guide to the Cloud computing IT model with a solid overview of concepts, business aspects, technical implications, benefits, challenges, and trends. Definitely a 'must read' for IT managers and enterprise architects considering adoption of this flexible, beneficial business model within their organization."

John Magnuson
Senior Staff Engineer
Lockheed Martin

"Melvin Greer has served as an innovative focal point for coordinating challenges that cross governmental agency boundaries and has provided best practices for Architecture & Infrastructure to CIOs, CTOs and CEAs nationally. Mr. Greer's methodologies and research have shaped the Federal Government's information management and technology agenda for the last 15 years. He has been on the cutting edge and forefront of Enterprise Architecture, Service Oriented Architecture and Internet computing. The Federal government is delivering results through expansion and adoption of digital, electronic government principles and best practices in managing information technology because of Mr. Greer's guidance and subject matter expertise. Through the implementation of these best practices, methodologies and principles, Mr. Greer has introduced to the government the ability to provide timely and accurate information to citizens and government decision makers while ensuring security and privacy for all".

Ken Tolson
Chief Operating Officer
Innovative Technology Lead
Emergency Technology Consortium

"This book offers the most comprehensive view of Cloud computing and SaaS on the market today. The author skillfully lays out a game plan for government and commercial entities alike looking to stay relevant in this burgeoning business paradigm."

Ken Brown
Program Account Executive
IBM Federal

"While the myths about Cloud computing, Software as a Service and the future of application systems continue to be spread by users, vendors, so-called IT gurus and the general Internet audience, some people are beginning to sort through the haystack and are pointing us in the right direction. Taking a series of myths and translating them into real-life terms, products and companies is one of the feats achieved by Melvin Greer in his new book. Whether you are looking for a roadmap to help steer your company in the right direction or simply trying to understand those concepts in more detail, if you start by reading this book, you will be starting off on the right foot."

Rob Martins
Chicago Business Unit Executive
Stefanini IT Solutions

"Melvin Greer dispels the myths of Cloud computing by taking a frank and candid look at the industry. He also provides concrete steps for successful implementation of Cloud computing."

Star Hill
Candidate
Princeton University Graduate Program

"Melvin Greer has taken the complexities of technology utilization (SaaS and Cloud Computing) and makes it a business multiplier that cannot be ignored."

Darold Hamlin
President and Executive Director
Emerging Technology Consortium

"Melvin Greer defines the discussion on the forces driving our future business needs in the new world of SaaS and Cloud Computing. We are on the cusp—the inflection point—of Web 2.0 Changing Everything. Mel Greer delineates the forces we all must consider in moving our businesses forward. Microsoft, Amazon, and Google have agilely defined the future of software; Mel Greer lays out the forces of change, and where they are likely to lead."

Michael I. Schwartz
Fellow
Lockheed Martin

ALSO BY MELVIN GREER

The Web Services and Service Oriented Architecture Revolution

For Maria Carmela and Stefan

Special Thanks to my Suocera Maria Serra Di Paolo

About the Author

Melvin Greer is Senior Research Engineer, SOA Chief Architect, and Director SOA Competency Center, Lockheed Martin, Advanced Technologies Office. With over 20 years of systems and software engineering experience, he functions as a principal investigator in advanced research studies. He significantly advances the body of knowledge in basic research and critical, highly advanced engineering and scientific disciplines. Mr. Greer holds membership as a Strategist on the Information Technology Association of America, Cloud Computing Committee and holds membership in the Government Cloud Computing Community of Interest.

In addition to his professional and investment roles, Mr. Greer is a Certified Enterprise Architect, Fellow and Adjunct Faculty at the Federal Enterprise Architects Institute, and member of International Monetary Fund / World Bank, Bretton Woods Committee. Mr. Greer is a frequent speaker at conferences and universities and is an accomplished author. His book "The Web Services and Service Oriented Architecture Revolution" has received wide acclaim.

Mr. Greer has held numerous senior leadership positions, helping global enterprises based in Germany, United Kingdom, and Brazil with their reengineering and transformational initiatives.

Mr. Greer received his Bachelor of Science degree in Computer Information Systems and Technology and his Master of Science in Information Systems from American University, Wash. D.C. He has also completed the Executive Leadership Program at Cornell University, Johnson Graduate School.

Foreword

A strategic inflection point is a time in the life of a business when its fundamentals are about to change. That change can mean an opportunity to rise to new heights; but it may just as likely signal the beginning of the end.

Strategic inflection points can be caused by technological change, but they are more than technological change. Competitors can cause them, but they are more than just competition. Strategic inflection points are full-scale changes in the way business is conducted so that simply adopting new technology or fighting the competition, as has been done in the past, may not be sufficient. They build up force such that organizations may have a hard time even putting a finger on what has changed, yet they know that something has. Let's not mince words: a strategic inflection point can be deadly when unattended to. Organizations that begin a decline as a result of large scale changes rarely recover their previous greatness.

Strategic inflection points do not always lead to disaster. When the way business is being conducted changes, it creates opportunities for players adept at operating in the new way. This can apply to newcomers or to incumbents, for whom a strategic inflection point may mean an opportunity for a new period of growth.

Over the last few years' industry has begun developing a model of information technology (IT) known as Cloud computing which includes Software as a Service (SaaS). This new model has reached an inflection point and will give users the choice to purchase IT as a service, as a complement to or in replacement of the traditional IT software/hardware infrastructure purchase. SaaS and Cloud computing have benefits for the economy, government, innovation, and energy efficiency and competitiveness.

CONTENTS

ILLUSTRATIONS

SOFTWARE AS A SERVICE INFLECTION POINT

USING CLOUD COMPUTING TO ACHIEVE BUSINESS AGILITY

INTRODUCTION

Software as a Service, SaaS, is a model for delivering software solutions to businesses and individuals where the software is owned, delivered, and managed by an external provider. It is a subset of the overarching umbrella of "Cloud computing" in which users access applications and data through the Web. Commercial businesses as well as governmental agencies, including the United States Postal Service and the Defense Information Systems Agency, are making the transition to a SaaS delivery model to help achieve cost reduction targets. Such transitions involve the evaluation of SaaS test programs aimed at meeting such requirements as data security and ownership, ease-of-use, rapid implementation, and decreased reliance on in-house IT resources. According to Ron Markezich, Corporate VP of Microsoft [1], customers of the SaaS model have saved anywhere from 10% to 80% on the cost of their infrastructure. A growing need for business agility with the potential for reducing operating costs drives the need for organizations to evaluate the SaaS model for future adoption and implementation as a user and/or as a provider.

This book educates senior executives, key decision makers and users on the concepts of SaaS and Cloud computing. It provides an evaluation framework that could be utilized to develop and execute a transition to Software as a Service as part of an enterprise system. Finally, it recommends how the SaaS model should be applied to achieve business agility.

ONE: INFLECTION POINT

An event that changes the way we think and act.

-Andy Grove, Founder of Intel

Inflection Point: The time when an organization makes a strategic decision to change its strategy to pursue a different direction and avoid the risk of decline. The term was coined by Andy Grove of Intel to describe the period of change that affects an organization's competitive position. It also describes the need for organizations to recognize and adapt to change.

An inflection point in business occurs when the old strategic picture dissolves and gives way to a new one. "Inflection point" is a term used in multiple disciplines including mathematics, engineering and business strategy to describe a point on a curve where the curvature changes from convex to concave. In business strategy, an inflection point is frequently used to describe a scenario where the dynamics of today's business situation significantly shift. In this case, the term inflection point indicates the point at which the business requirements needed to compete significantly shift. It may not mean that the fundamentals of today's model no longer work, but rather that there is a transition occurring, when a new set of rules is being defined to set the stage for a new and different competitive landscape. Managing this transition is the ultimate challenge for industry leaders.

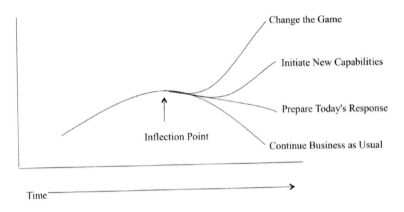

Change the Game

Initiate New Capabilities

Prepare Today's Response

Inflection Point

Continue Business as Usual

Time

Figure 1: The Inflection Point

The experience of a wide array of industries, from airlines to entertainment to retail, indicates that new leaders emerge when companies recognize the opportunity created by an inflection point – that is, performance differentiation in the future. In making the transition, organizations must continue to operate in the world of today, while preparing for the world of tomorrow. That challenge presents a host of dilemmas including:

- How aggressively should they pursue the future model?
- Should they should lead or follow?
- How can they overcome reluctance to change?
- Should the capabilities be enhanced or built?

To understand how we have reached this Software as a Service inflection point and how organizations might achieve the business agility that SaaS and Cloud computing promise, we should begin by looking at some of the drivers behind the SaaS phenomenon and what the trends tell us about their future capability.

There are three primary concerns with the current software model that is driving us toward the SaaS inflection point:

- Upfront financial commitment: Software and ancillary services, such as implementation, integration, customization, testing, maintenance, training and overtime upgrading, can add a multiple of five to seven times license fees during the lifetime of an application. This concern is exacerbated by the common lack of control over ongoing costs after the deployment.

- Unused software: A great deal of software remains unused. One of the reasons software becomes "shelf ware" is the overselling by software vendor sales forces, who often use discounts as an incentive to encourage large upfront purchases for future potential need.

- Complexity of the software: The complexity of much of the software and its lack of user friendliness often leads to poor utilization and value realization.

For these and other reasons, vendors are using new technologies — the Internet, service oriented architecture and Web 2.0 — to develop newer, more cost-effective delivery models and advanced software solutions. The movement toward SaaS has been germinating for many years and, after some missteps, has finally reached an inflection that will make a meaningful impact on the IT industry. Gartner Research[2] forecasts that by 2011, 25% of *new* business software will be delivered as SaaS.

Managing an inflection point necessitates operating concurrently in two worlds—the world of today and the world of tomorrow. There is no single approach to developing a strategy to accomplish this. Since much depends on a company's product portfolio, its organizational readiness and its tolerance for risk, transition timeframes can vary from organization to organization. Any inflection point, however, provides the opportunity to erect the building blocks of high performance and achieve differentiation.

3

A company in an industry at an inflection point can set a trajectory toward industry leadership.

To achieve success, there are three general strategies that organizations should consider when developing a plan that manages an inflection point:

- Ready today's model by improving critical aspects of the current business model in an attempt to slow declining performance.
- Institute new capabilities to drive competitive advantage and boost performance.
- Change the game by defining new business practices that will create a new performance trajectory.

Variations in inflection point strategies do and should exist. It is the role of executives in each company to recognize the mix of strategies/imperatives that makes sense, given the unique set of challenges and resources it faces. Executives who lead today will win tomorrow by defining their own inflection point strategy. The strategy should be based on a viewpoint of the future industry landscape. It should evaluate current capabilities and portfolios, define risk tolerance and thus the degree of aggressiveness with which to pursue the strategy and create a change agenda and corresponding set of imperatives. Successful companies will align the leadership team around this change agenda, fast-track their chosen imperatives, evaluate and reconfigure their talent base, and create a program structure robust enough to manage the ongoing transformation journey to high performance.

Two: The Significance of Business Agility

Business Agility is an organization's ability to respond to change. If the organization cannot respond well to change, it can lose competitive advantage or even cease to exist. In a world where change is more rapid and becoming less predictable, increased agility is undoubtedly critical to corporate survival. Rapid and impactful change also often presents important new opportunities. If an enterprise is less agile than its competitors, it is the competitor who will capitalize on new opportunities and grow.

There are a number of drivers forcing business agility. First, there is an increase in interconnectedness: email, Web, digital supply chains and mobile devices are linking us to each other in real time. Second, there are "macro" changes. These include changing market conditions, new regulations and political situations in various parts of the world that impact business. Third, there is the growing role of information and data to improve corporate productivity. When a new medication, a new nanotechnology manufacturing technique or an innovative marketing strategy is developed, information technology is being used to increase productivity. Finally, there is profitability. Organizations are under more pressure than ever to be profitable — while, at the same time, they are faced with new challenges in achieving increased profitability.

To achieve business agility, organizations are focusing on four main areas – the components of agility: people, processes, strategy and technology. These components are inextricably linked: if the ball is dropped on one aspect of agility, the others will suffer. For example, an organization's employees may understand how to respond to change and are motivated to do so, but if technology does not give them the information they need to observe change, they will not be able to make good decisions. If agility is built into all four components, a "virtual cycle" is created that will feed onto itself and ensure an ongoing, dynamic response to change as it occurs.

Quantifying agility involves the use of frameworks; these can be used by organizations to measure their level of agility and business value. An example of an agility framework is the Agility Quotient (AQ) tool developed by Microsoft and Gartner. The Agility Quotient tool can help organizations understand their ability to sense and respond to change as well as benchmarks their performance against industry peers. It analyzes their level of awareness, flexibility and productivity during change and outlines tangible steps to improve. If an organization takes steps to improve agility (for example, by upgrading its IT infrastructure), it can then use investment tools such as the Microsoft Rapid Economic Justification (REJ) framework to understand the value derived from its IT investments. Many organizations have used the AQ tool to identify their level of organizational agility and to determine how to use technology to achieve an optimal state.

To survive, enterprises need a rock-solid, streamlined IT environment; but to win, they must transform their IT investment into a corporate advantage — one that drives revenue and growth and opens new markets and opportunities. Today's business climate requires a constantly evolving IT strategy that responds to new opportunities and threats on the fly. While the fundamentals of IT — reliability, availability, security and manageability — are still crucial, rapid results are mandatory for business success. There is little room for a trade-off between reliability and agility — organizations need both.

Experts agree on the central role that agility plays. According to Gartner[3], "Progressive companies have adopted workplace agility as a competitive imperative." Giga calls agility a "critical element to deal with continuing innovation." Agility must characterize the business itself as well as the IT infrastructure and applications on which it depends. Research from META Group indicates that "during the operational life of complex, highly integrated systems, the largest and fastest-growing total cost-of-ownership (TCO) factor is change (i.e., adaptability). Users must continue to emphasize adaptability as their primary design goal to deliver lower TCO."

The essence of business agility is defined by John Oleson in "Pathways to Agility,"[4] as the ability to respond with ease to the unexpected. It means that the unexpected has been anticipated and the capability has been built so that the response can occur with ease."

An agile business can:

- Understand market dynamics and anticipate customer needs.

- Make faster decisions through better access to information.

- Gain access to critical business information wherever and whenever required.

- Design, introduce or modify business services and processes.

- Automatically deploy or re-deploy resources based on dynamically evolving business requirements.

- Maintain and improve customer service levels.

Unfortunately, most organizations are more familiar with these symptoms:

- Struggling to deploy new features because of the risk of business disruption.

- Supporting end-of-life or outdated proprietary systems and custom applications.

- Reaching performance ceilings, yet being unable to take advantage of next-generation technologies.

- Paying for underutilized assets that cannot be re-used for other purposes.

Today's business environment is one of rapid and continuous change; one that is marked by an increasing dependence on advanced software capability that will enable the performance of a growing number of business tasks. In this environment, the time and cost to transform information systems to respond to environmental change and the strategies developed to address that change could be a competitive advantage or disadvantage. In effect, information systems agility is becoming a larger component of enterprise agility at a time when enterprise agility is becoming more critical to enterprise success. However, many CEOs and corporate board members view existing information systems and corporate culture as primary inhibitors to strategic change. Enterprise architecture can improve information systems by creating agile advanced software methodologies, by improving development and testing environments, and by enhancing SaaS and Cloud computing skills. However, the greatest potential gains in information systems agility will come from using enterprise architecture to develop and transmit agility-centric requirements, principles and models for information architecture to every systems development and acquisition decision. A well formed SaaS and Cloud computing inflection point strategy will be based on a strategic business vision that is derived from the enterprise's strategy and external drivers, enablers and inhibitors of change. The strategic business vision will be based not only on known and forecast process and information requirements defined by business units, but also on enterprise-level "engineering requirements". In today's world of rapid and continuous change, agility is, more often than not, paramount among these engineering requirements. In an environment in which CEOs and executive teams must plan business strategy on a multi scenario basis, it is difficult for business-unit project sponsors and IT professionals to forecast process and information requirements with the accuracy necessary to define information systems process and data structures beyond the immediate future. Therefore, because forecasting requirements will not result in stable future-state information architectures, designing for agility is necessary to maintain alignment with a rapidly and continuously changing business environment. The focus on business agility is a primary driver for the rapid response and flexibility associated with the software delivery models associated with Cloud computing and SaaS, and the main reason we have reached an inflection point with regards to their adoption.

THREE: CLOUD COMPUTING AND SAAS

Any significant discussion on SaaS will include the concept of Cloud computing. Cloud computing is a style of computing, where massively scalable IT-enabled capabilities are delivered "as a service" to external customers using Internet technologies. This is different from traditional computing internal models and has distinguishing attributes — such as multi-tenant and massive scale characteristics — when compared to other traditional hosting models. Elastically scalable Cloud computing resources are distributed dynamically and are redistributed on demand in metered quantity and quality. Delivery "as a service" implies that the base of the resources is off-premises relative to the consumer of the service — that is, the term "as a service" implies that it is off-premises.

Computing off-premises is a long-standing enterprise practice. Since the 1970s service providers have been hosting business applications on behalf of enterprises that chose not to own a mainframe computer. During the past four decades, as the prevailing computing models evolved and new platform technologies have emerged, off-premises computing have evolved as well. Today, an observer can find many models of off-premises computing in operation at the same time, often employed by the same IT organization. In most cases, the distinctions among the models are subtle: partly technical and partly business-related. In fact, multiple models that are named differently for historic reasons may overlap in many characteristics.

To clear away the resulting confusion, the figure below details a symbolic diagram and a set of common-sense definitions. Each model is discussed in greater detail and with greater precision. These models should not be treated as strict definitions, rather as "common sense" or "center of gravity" indications of the essentials of each category.

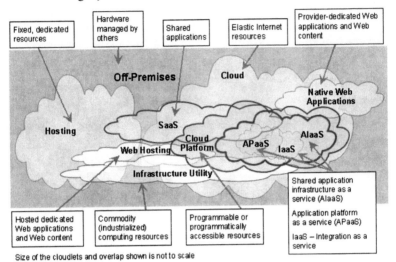

Figure 2: Off-Premise Offerings

Off-Premises

The service, including the application and the data, resides on hardware that the user organization does not own. This is a relative position: what are off-premises offerings for some are on-premises for someone else. Not owning the resource implies that there is no upfront one-time acquisition cost, but rather that the provider is paid for the service on a recurring (subscription) basis. These characteristics apply to all models discussed here.

In the off-premises IT scenario, there are always two parties involved: the one that provides the resources (the provider) and the one that "rents" them (the user organization).

Hosting

Off-premises computing resources are allocated exclusively by the provider to a particular user organization. If a provider has such an arrangement with multiple user organizations, then each will have its own exclusive computing resources from hardware up. There is minimal or no sharing of capabilities or costs among user organizations.

Cloud

Off-premises computing resources are allocated to applications and/or user organizations with elasticity: just-in-time with on-demand and metered quantity and quality (advanced capability). To fulfill this requirement, the provider must have resources that substantially exceed the average use patterns. Therefore, mature cloud environments are characterized by massive scalability.

Web Hosting

The application or content is hosted by one entity (the provider) and owned exclusively by one other (the user organization). The resources are off-premises, relative to the user organization, and are dedicated to it. Access to the resources is available via the Web (that is, by HTTP). Some Web hosting uses fully fixed resources allocated exclusively to a paying user organization (as in classic hosting). In other cases, Web hosting is optimized, and some underlying resources may be shared with some degree of elasticity. Thus, some Web hosting extends into the cloud by virtue of being elastic, although the resources in use remain dedicated to one user organization.

Native Web Applications

These are Web-based applications in which the two parties are the provider (for example, Google Search or Orbitz.com) and the individual. The resources (that is, the applications and content) are off-premises, relative to the individual. The resources are dedicated to only one user organization (the provider) and are on-premises relative to it. In some notable cases, such as Google, Yahoo and Amazon, the provider offers multiple applications and uses elastic, massively scalable methods for dynamically allocating shared resources to its many applications. Thus, these are native cloud applications. In other cases, such as most e-commerce sites, the resources are fixed and have a limited scale capacity. These are not part of the cloud, although they are certainly Web offerings.

Infrastructure Utility
These are off-premises computing resources that are self-contained, programmatically accessible and approaching commodity status. The choice of provider is nearly irrelevant and is based on price, performance and quality, but not on features and capabilities.

Software as a Service
SaaS involves off-premises resources, typically business applications, offered in a one-to-many model: multiple user organizations using the same application. Despite the shared model, each user organization experiences as if it were the only entity using the application. The one-to-many model can be implemented through multi-tenancy or isolated tenancy. Multi-tenancy implies elasticity — thus, multitenant SaaS is part of Cloud computing. Isolated tenancy allocates fixed isolated resources to each user organization — thus, it is a form of hosting.

Cloud Platform
This is a platform in the cloud for building new and composite applications, processes, information sources and services. Cloud platform technology includes programmable environments and provides programmatic access to cloud-based computing resources at multiple levels, including system infrastructure services, application services and application infrastructure services. For example, a cloud application is typically accessed via its user interfaces (UIs). If it also exposes programmatic UIs, then it becomes a cloud platform, because it is a programmatically accessible resource usable for new development.

Cloud platform technologies may be used in mixed on-premises/ off-premises applications or in pure cloud applications. Gartner uses the terms "cloud platform," "Web platform" and "cloud/ Web platform" interchangeably. There are multiple cloud/Web platforms.

Application Infrastructure as a Service

Application infrastructure is synonymous with the broad definition of middleware, including platforms, integration and business process management. When enhanced with multitenant elasticity to enable its use off-premises, application infrastructure is offered as a service and is a key cloud platform technology.

Application Platform as a Service

This is an in-cloud platform for the development and deployment of new cloud application software — analogous to an on-premises application server, with added multitenant elasticity and other cloud-enabling features. It is a type of cloud platform technology and a type of the broader Application Infrastructure as a Service.

Infrastructure as a Service

This is a multitenant platform for off-premises integration, which is analogous to an on-premise integration suite. A typical use pattern is a multi enterprise integration and interoperability exchange enabling user organizations to establish secure and trusted connections to their business partners, suppliers and other external parties. It is a type of cloud platform technology and a type of the broader Application Infrastructure as a Service.

Cloud computing is an alternate delivery and acquisition model for IT-related services. It shifts the way purchasers of IT products and services contract with vendors, and the way those vendors deliver their wares. The cloud can be defined as an abstract environment that makes IT services (or capabilities) accessible

15

through the Internet to anyone who has the wherewithal to buy and use them. This ubiquitous delivery of IT, much like the Industrial Revolution, will alter the way many organizations approach the delivery of business services enabled by IT.

Figure 1. Cloud Computing's Distinguishing Attributes

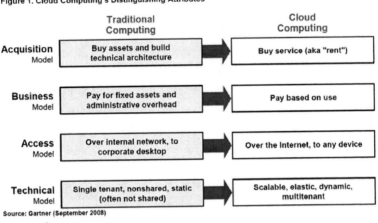

Source: Gartner (September 2008)

Figure 3: Cloud computing Attributes

Myths are rampant in the IT industry and it is no different with Cloud computing. These are issues that generally relate to attempts by vendors to align cloud messaging to the historical products and services they provide. However, some myths are a general misunderstanding and hype about the cloud. Cloud computing is not an architecture or infrastructure; it is an abstraction of the relationship between the consumers and the providers of services. There are many different approaches to delivering Cloud computing. These approaches may not be creating different clouds; they tend to feed services into the one public cloud.

Much of this cloud approach is not new, but what is new is the change in mindset, involvement and availability of technology to be used by masses of people who care about what they can do with the technology instead of how the technology is implemented. Not everything will become Cloud computing, because many projects will require a level of privacy, performance, or uniqueness that cannot yet be supported through the public cloud.

Common use of Cloud computing is associated with service offerings centering on a few basic areas:

- Infrastructure as a service (IaaS): Web-centric infrastructure for storage, compute capability and other capabilities, leveraging distinct services such as Amazon Web Services (for example, Heavy.com uses Amazon's EC2 with other cloud services like Akamai).

- Application platform as a service (APaaS): A complete infrastructure for applications, leveraging services like Google App Engine and Force.com (the non application part of salesforce.com's cloud service offerings). Many, like Morph AppSpace and eXchange (www. morphexchange.com), sit on top of Amazon's web services (IaaS) offerings.

- Software as a service (SaaS): Complete application capability leveraging services (such as salesforce.com or Google Docs or Gmail) that are less enterprise differentiating and that are increasingly based on open-source software.

- Service Oriented Architecture (SOA) Interfaces: Authentication, payment and other capabilities increasingly offered to augment other internally provided applications or solutions leveraging services like Amazon Flexible Payments Service or PayPal Express Checkout. These are not complete applications, but parts — usually accessed via service-oriented architecture (SOA) interface technologies.

- Batch and parallel processing loads (batch): Serial file processing — for example, GigaVox Media and its IT Conversations network, which leverages many of Amazon's IaaS services (as described in Doug Kaye's blog Blogarithms: Amazon for Infrastructure on-Demand). Printing services, file conversion services and so on are common opportunities.

SaaS consists primarily of business applications deployed off-premise relative to the enterprise. The applications look "normal" and, as far as the user is concerned, differ from on-premise applications mostly in the way they are paid for (subscription per use versus perpetual license per power unit), as well as in the way they are supported (out of reach and not a burden for the enterprise's own IT). However, for SaaS-style applications to make good business sense for application providers, their internal architecture must be adjusted as well. Multiple enterprise capabilities are deployed in shared-resource environments to reduce, if not eliminate, the waste of resource capacity. The cost of adding or removing a user organization is generally minimal, especially if the vendors support hundreds or even thousands of such user organizations. The underlying virtualization technology must be of a high caliber, since such shared environments might routinely cover tens of thousands of concurrent users.

Applications require an underlying platform whether they are on-premises or "in the cloud". Most of such platforms used for SaaS today are internal, although vendors such as Salesforce.com are also offering their application platforms for third-party application development and deployment. A SaaS-enabled application platform (SEAP) can be a whole IT infrastructure "in the cloud", allowing an organization to develop, test, deploy, manage and even sell their business application to others, with minimal on-site technology investment. The Cloud computing business model options and the underlying technical capabilities differ from established enterprise business model, thus creating distinct business opportunities and advanced software computing options for enterprises to consider.

THE BENEFITS OF CLOUD COMPUTING

Cloud computing makes it possible to deliver software applications remotely or locally on a private cloud, and deliver the application to a large number of users. This creates important advantages.

- Cost: Infrastructure is purchased as a service, resulting in savings through shared infrastructure, reducing redundancies, realizing economies of scale, limiting license requirements, exploiting hardware virtualization and using the best platform for the applications requirements.

- Agility: Cloud applications can typically be implemented quickly (from a couple days to a couple months) and deployed instantly and simultaneously to thousands of users in different locations around the world. Since Cloud computing providers update their own platforms, users do not have to take on this responsibility themselves.

- Ease of Use: Some Cloud computing applications are modeled after consumer browser based web applications or after interface models that are familiar from leading software applications, so they tend to be intuitive and easy to use. Both user adoption rates and customer satisfaction rates are typically very high.

- Green: Even though Cloud computing data centers consume substantial amounts of power, their net consumption of energy is far below that of numerous computing installations replicated for individual organizations. Additionally, this consumption is declining because of more energy efficient platform technologies and virtualization technology.

- Business Continuity/Availability: With enterprise data strategies in Cloud computing, enterprises and government agencies can access that data anytime and from anywhere, which enhances data availability and business continuity capabilities. In addition, because of Cloud computing virtualization agility, continuity of operations no longer needs to be budgeted as a separate entity because it is now an integral element of the business solutions formulation with no additional cost being incurred.

Cloud computing allows individuals, organizations and government access to processing and storage computing resources over the Internet without having to buy, deploy, maintain or upgrade complex information technology systems. Cloud computing enables users to extend the functionality and value of their existing IT investments as well as gives them additional choices, allowing them to run applications and store data remotely or locally, depending on their needs. Although there is a lively debate on the exact definition of Cloud computing, there is consensus around four basic elements being a part of Cloud computing:

Offsite Data Centers – Any cloud service must have elements to it that take place in an offsite or, in the case of a private cloud, in a shared on-site data center. Services may be provided completely in offsite data centers, within a company or government's own data centers in the form of a private cloud or as collaboration between a data center and traditional IT services on an individual's computer. As a result, the user does not have to install or maintain a local copy of the software or invest in IT infrastructure – instead they have a choice among using, replacing or complementing existing IT infrastructure with the cloud service.

Internet, Network or Wide Area Network (WAN) Access – Traditionally, applications are designed to be accessed over the public Internet. Users typically access the applications with a web browser. Cloud computing applications accessed via public or private clouds, are standards-based, independent of the specific hardware and software implementation that exists on any one computer.

Pay Per Use Services – Cloud products are purchased as a service, usually on a per-user or per-usage basis, rather than a one-time license.

Massive Scalability_- Applications can be delivered to thousands or millions of users and the environment allows for flexibility to encompass varying workloads and requirements. Computing resources can be allocated dynamically to deliver on-demand resources that can expand and contract as needed. Additionally, business and government no longer have to maintain surplus capacity to support their business solutions as demand expands and contracts – instead, IT solutions are delivered just in time.

For businesses, Cloud computing has the potential to provide large productivity gains because companies of all sizes can use Internet platforms to process data they have traditionally managed on their own or to extend the functionality and value of their existing IT investments. For entrepreneurs, Cloud computing is a pathway to innovation because it can enable start-up companies to develop, run and sell their products on global Internet platforms at very low cost. For government, Cloud computing promises can reduce the risk, cost, and delay associated with information technology projects while allowing for more collaboration with the public.

EMERGING TRENDS IN CLOUD COMPUTING AND NEXT STEPS

Cloud computing is an emerging business, solution and technical set of capabilities. Organizations of all types are investigating the trends, tools, vendors and business options, looking for immediate impact and returns. The focus on business agility is driving the continued focus on alternative advanced software, data center, and technology delivery capabilities. A review of the current trends and a short list of investigative next steps will assist organizations in the development of a cloud computing strategic plan.

The emerging trends in Cloud computing include:

- Consumer demand for Web-delivered services is growing.
- Software as a Service is only the tip of the iceberg; it is envisioned that soon everything will be a service.
- Internal private clouds will proliferate quickly; internal service delivery will guarantee safety.
- The cloud is already upsetting technology sales models.
- The cloud will upset economic models.

Due to the above trends, software vendors will be forced to introduce cloud platforms even if they are not ready. In addition, user organizations will have to learn to manage service contracts rather than manage product licenses.

The executive next steps in Cloud computing include:
- **Today** (Monday morning):
    - Begin to catalog what cloud services are available (from Amazon to Zoho) and consider what their use will mean to your (or your customers') interests.

- *Direct emerging technology teams to evaluate Cloud computing and Web/cloud platform technologies and explore various adoption scenarios.*
- **Near Future** (the next 12 months):
  - Begin an evaluation of your technology legacy and how modernization would affect them.
  - *Demand that your technology providers explain how Web/cloud platform models will impact their offering and pricing strategies.*
  - *Determine whether the cloud will ultimately be robust enough to meet your business goals.*
- **Long Term** (3-5 years):
  - *Determine if, when and how the enterprise should expose its information, application and/or processes to others as Web/cloud platform services.*
  - *Determine when or if you would be able to offer services to the cloud or whether your role will be as a service consumer.*

Four: Public Cloud Offerings

There is a variety of Cloud computing services offered to public enterprises as well as different types of virtualization services from major providers such as Microsoft, Amazon, and Google. These services include Azure Services Platform, Google App Engine, and Amazon Web Services. A brief high-level overview of the architecture will be introduced along with the types of tools that adopters will use to consume these services. Lastly, a feature-by-feature comparison from each of the major public cloud providers is submitted including an analysis of the various offerings.

Azure Services Platform

The Azure Services Platform is Microsoft's first implementation of Cloud computing. It is relatively new; its debut was announced during the Professional Developers Conference on October 27th, 2008.[5] The platform is hosted in Microsoft's data centers and offers an operating system (OS) and a set of services that developers can use to build applications that run in the cloud (described below). At the moment, the platform only supports applications that are built using managed code in the .NET Framework. However, in the near future, Azure will have the capability to support more programming languages and development environments.[6] Although they are limited in language support at this time, the services are fully interoperable and meet industry standards such as Representational State Transfer (REST) and Simple Object Access Protocol (SOAP).

The following is a description of the operating system and the platform's set of services.

Windows Azure Operating System

- Computation Service
  - Can run ASP.NET Web apps or .NET code in the cloud
  - Service hosting with IIS 7.0 and .NET Framework 3.5 SP1
  - Flexible Code Access Security policies
  - Logging support and local scratch storage
  - Web portal that allows users to scale, deploy, and upgrade services
- Storage Services
  - Blobs, tables, and queues
  - Authenticated access
  - Access to data using REST services

.NET Services
- Access Control
  - Federated Identity and Access Control can federate with 3rd party Secure Token services. Trust can be setup through a web UI or API calls. Supports Active Directory. Service Bus endpoint can be secured through web UI or rule sets.
  - Supports multiple credentials (e.g. X.509 certificates, Windows Live IDs, traditional username and passwords, managed and personal cards).
- Service Bus
  - The .NET Service Bus is Microsoft's implementation of the Enterprise Service Bus (ESB). However unlike the traditional ESB, the Service Bus is not limited to managing on-premise applications. It is capable of

operating on an Internet scope in Microsoft's highly-scalable data centers. One of the core features of the .NET Service Bus is a centralized, highly load-balanced relay service that supports different transport protocols and Web services standards such as SOAP, WS*, and REST. The Service Bus supports all types of programming environments however it is optimized for Windows Communication Foundation services.[7]

- Workflow Services

  - Based on Windows Workflow Foundation, it offers a lightweight service orchestration with the capability to define, design, manage, and scale activities.

Structured Query Language Data Services

- SQL Data Services provides a database in the cloud where on-premise and cloud applications can store and access data on servers in the Microsoft Data Centers. Data can be accessed using current web standard interfaces such as SOAP and REST. Although SQL Data Services is built on Microsoft SQL Server, it does not use the traditional relational interface. Each data item is stored in a name, value, and type property in a hierarchical model. This model is fit for a cloud environment because it carries the advantage of better scalability, availability, and reliability.[8]

Live Services

- Applications work together with the Live Framework to synchronize Live Services data across desktop, laptop, and devices. An example of an application that takes advantage of this capability is Live Mesh. Live Mesh allows users to add their desktop machines and mobile devices to the Live Desktop cloud to keep all of their data in sync.

GOOGLE APP ENGINE

The Google App Engine offers the capability of running web applications on Google's infrastructure. It supports dynamic web applications, storage, scaling, load balancing, and Application Programming Interfaces for authenticating users. The development environment can simulate Google App Engine on a local machine, before deploying to the cloud. Applications developed using the Google App Engine API are limited to only the Python programming language.

The Sandbox

Applications run in a secure environment that provides limited access to the underlying operating system. These limitations allow App Engine to distribute web requests for the application across multiple servers, and start and stop servers to meet traffic demands. The sandbox isolates your application in its own secure, reliable environment that is independent of the hardware, operating system and physical location of the web server.[9]

The Data Store

The Data Store is a distributed and scalable data store where users can perform queries and transactions on data objects known as entities. It uses a distributed architecture to manage and scale large data sets. The Python API allows users to define a structure for data objects, or "entities" through their data modeling interface.

App Engine Services

- URL Fetch – This service allows communication with other applications and access to web resources by fetching the URL. Some use cases would include communicating with web services or retrieving Really

Simple Syndication (RSS) feeds. There are some limitations to fetches where accessing any URL other than port 80 or 443 is restricted.

- Mail – An email service for sending and retrieving emails message from your application.

AMAZON WEB SERVICES (AWS)

AWS is the most mature out of the three cloud offerings. They also cover the four central elements of a web-scale infrastructure: storage, computing, messaging, and datasets. They are designed to work together with high availability and scalability.

Simple Storage Service (S3)

- S3 provides a web service interface for storing and retrieving data for applications, personal or enterprise data. It can also distribute large contents of media. Data is stored using the concepts of *Buckets*. Buckets can be seen as folder, directories, or file systems. Objects that are stored in buckets are accessible through the URL (e.g. http://foo.s3.amazonaws. com). A bucket can have an unlimited number of objects, and each object has a 5 GB limit. Each object is identified using a unique key which is the name of the object (e.g. http://foo.s3.amazonaws.com/bar. doc).[10]

Elastic Cloud Compute (EC2)

- EC2 allows users to setup virtual instances while configuring computing requirements on the fly. The framework contains Amazon Machine Images (AMI) which are packaged server environments based on Linux. Users can choose between private, public, and paid images. Users can scale virtual instances that use the AMI as a template. Each instance can be based on 32-bit or 64-bit platforms ranging anywhere from small instances to extra large instances. Users can control access to these instances by configuring the security groups and security pairs.[11]

Simple Queue Service (SQS)

- SQS is a scalable and reliable messaging framework that allows you to integrate applications that are decoupled. Messages can contain text up to 8 KB in size and will stay in the queue until an application retrieves them, however SQS will delete messages that have not been retrieved for four days.[12]

SimpleDB (SDB)

- SDB is a Web services for storing, processing, and querying structured datasets. Similar to the design of Microsoft's and Google's cloud solution, SDB is not a traditional relational database. This is because SDB is built to be highly available and scalable where data can be retrieved using unique keyed values. Each keyed value needs a unique item name, where each item can hold up to 256 key-value pairs. The item names are required to be unique because each item is partitioned into domains.

FEATURE COMPARISON

Below is a side-by-side comparison of the important features from the major vendors that were discussed above.

	Microsoft	Amazon	Google
Availability	In preview – Community Technology Preview stages	Mature (though recently added Windows support is in Beta)	Preview Release Beta

	Microsoft	Amazon	Google
Computing Architecture	Applications run on Windows Azure in the cloud. Developers publish their code to the front-end (web Virtual Machine) and the back-end (worker VM). Each VM runs on Windows Server 2008 which can be scaled to the developer's needs.	You follow their workflow to create an Amazon Machine Image. They allow you to create an instance based on most common Linux distributions. Amazon recently opened more doors to allow you to create Microsoft Windows Server and SQL Server instances.[13]	Applications run in Google's sandbox with limited access to the underlying operating system. Developers upload their code to the App Engine which was written using the Python programming language.
Load Balancing	Yes	Yes	Yes
Supported Languages	Supports applications and services that were built using the .NET Framework. Microsoft has announced plans to support other languages in the near future.	Supports any language installed on developer's box (e.g. Java, C, C++, PHP) Also welcomes C# due to the new support for Windows instances.	Applications must be developed in Python version 2.5.2 or higher or Django (a high-level Python Web framework).

	Microsoft	Amazon	Google
Storage	Yes, through SQL Database Service (a cloud-deployed database service). Stores information in BLOBS or other standardized fields.	Yes, through Simple Storage Service (S3)	Yes, through the App Engine Datastore. Stores data objects in *entities*, which contain one or more named properties, named values of one of several supported types. Also backed by BigTable.
Queues	Yes	Yes, through Simple Queue Service (SQS)	No
Integration with Services	Yes • Live Services, • Live Mesh • Access control services • workflow services • services bus	No	Yes • authentication services • e-mail • calendar • contacts • documents • pictures • spreadsheets
Hosted in vendor's Data Center	Yes	Yes	Yes

	Microsoft	Amazon	Google
Development tools	Yes, the Microsoft Windows Azure Software Development Kit provides developers with API's, tools, and documents needed to develop applications. Also provides integration tools with Visual Studio. It is only limited to .NET languages, but will support more in the near future.	No, Amazon supports all platforms.	Yes, the Google App Engine SDK simulates the App Engine environment so developers can test before uploading the code.

ANALYSIS OF THE CLOUD OFFERINGS

Based on the comparison of the three major cloud providers, we can see that they support the major requirements for a Cloud computing solution such as load balancing, computing, storage, and security. However, out of the three, the Google App Engine does not seem to provide the required set of capabilities needed to meet an enterprise's Cloud computing needs. Although Google is known and has been very successful in taking simplistic approaches, the Google App Engine falls slightly below par from its competitor's offerings.

One of the major features that the App Engine is currently missing is background processing. This is a handicap for application developers who want to partition their program into different instances. For example, a video surveillance software system would need the front-end process to display and record motion JPEGs from an Internet Protocol camera while a back-end process is needed to trigger an alert if motion is detected. Another major feature that the Google App Engine is missing is message queues. This is required for developers who want decouple their applications and develop a lightweight solution for communication without having to resort to the heavier web-services. The last constraint from the Google App Engine is the limitation in language: the developers must write their applications in Python.

Although Google is relatively new in the Cloud computing market, it offers a set of stable cloud services that is built from its successful existing resources. For example, the App Engine Datastore is backed by BigTable, which is their distributed storage platform. It has been very successful in supporting their YouTube architecture by storing and serving billions of thumbnail images for their videos. GAE also offers integration with their existing services such as their popular maps, mail, and calendar applications.

On the other hand Microsoft Windows Azure offers a broad platform of services with the enterprise developer in mind. Their platform offers a "one-click" publishing tool to send applications to their cloud when using the Azure Services SDK or Azure Tools for Visual Studio 2008. Microsoft sees the importance in background processing which is why they have built their publishing model around web-roles and worker-roles (or background role). They have also made scaling instances just as simple as their publishing, where developers can add machines with the click of a button. Although Microsoft has covered a wide spectrum of services, developers are still limited in language selection. At the moment, only manage code (.NET code) is supported.

Amazon has been on the cloud market the longest and is continuing to improve its services to meet compatibility and enterprise standards. For example in August of 2008, Amazon released Elastic Block Store, a service within their EC2. It provides off instance storage and offers improved durability, reliability, and expandability. This would also benefit those who have multiple instances and need to share a virtual store.

After analyzing all cloud offerings, it is still early to determine which provider will be the enterprise choice in the future markets of Cloud computing. Even though a cloud provider may have a capability that their competitor lacks, the competitor will eventually realize the demands for it and strive to meet those needs. For example, Google has recently announced in their roadmap plans to add background processing and messaging in their App Engine.[14] Also not too long ago, Amazon introduced support for Windows instances in their EC2 platform. Finally Microsoft will soon support unmanaged code in the Azure Services Platform.

Future Cloud computing capabilities from these major companies will eventually converge (just like popular programming languages such as C# and Java) and in the end, the enterprise choice will be will be based on cost and consumer-to-provider relationships. Until then, we can only select the offering that comes closest to fulfilling our current requirements.

Five: Cloud Computing Privacy and Confidentiality

Cloud computing has significant implications for the privacy of personal information as well as for the confidentiality of business and governmental information. A principal goal is to identify privacy and confidentiality issues that may be of interest or concern to Cloud computing participants. The World Privacy Form, "Privacy in the Clouds" report[15] that emphasis on and expansion of Cloud computing warrants a more careful look at its actual and potential privacy and confidentiality consequences.

A considerable amount of Cloud computing technology is already being used and developed in various flavors (e.g., private, public, internal, external, and vertical). Not all types of Cloud computing raise the same privacy and confidentiality risks. Some believe that much of the computing activity occurring today entirely on computers owned and controlled locally by users will shift to "the cloud" in the future. Whether this will turn out to be the case is uncertain and not especially important here. The continuing development and maturation of Cloud computing services however, is an undeniable reality.

Cloud computing services exist in many variations, including data storage sites, video websites, tax preparation websites, personal health record websites, photography websites, social networking websites, and many more. Any information stored locally on a computer could be stored in a cloud, including email, word processing documents, spreadsheets, videos, health records, photographs, tax or other financial information, business plans, PowerPoint presentations, accounting information, advertising campaigns, sales numbers, appointment calendars, address books, and more. The entire contents of a user's storage device may be stored with a single cloud provider or with many cloud providers. Whenever an individual, a business, a government agency, or other entity shares information in the cloud, privacy or confidentiality questions may arise.

A typical information exchange in Cloud computing occurs when a user shares information with the cloud provider. Can any and all information be legally shared in a cloud service? With Cloud computing, many factors affect the answer to this fundamental question. The shortest answer to the question, however, is that for some information and for some users, sharing may be illegal, may be limited in some ways, or may affect the status or protections of the information shared.

Generally, an individual is free to share his or her personal information with a cloud provider. For a business, disclosing the personal information of customers or employees, or other business information to a cloud provider is often unrestricted by law because no privacy law or other law applies. For example, privacy laws do not cover most marketing records in the United States. Even when privacy laws apply to particular categories of customer or employee information, disclosure to a cloud provider may not be restricted.

For a federal agency, various laws may have bearing on the decision to employ a cloud provider. For example, the Privacy Act of 1974 imposes standards for the collection, maintenance, use, and disclosure of personal information. The use of Cloud computing for personal information held by a federal agency may violate the Privacy Act of 1974, especially if there is no contractual arrangement between the agency and the cloud provider. If a Cloud provider offers services to the public on behalf of agencies, other Privacy Act requirements may apply, as may security obligations under various federal laws and policies.

Federal record management and disposal laws may also be relevant.

PRIVACY AND CONFIDENTIALITY FINDINGS

Cloud computing has significant implications for the privacy of personal information as well as for the confidentiality of business and governmental information.

There are multiple and complex privacy and confidentiality issues that may be of interest or concern to Cloud computing participants. While storage of user data on remote servers is not a new activity, the current emphasis on and expansion of Cloud computing warrants a more careful look at the privacy and confidentiality consequences.

A user's privacy and confidentiality risks vary significantly with the terms of service and privacy policy established by the cloud provider.

Those risks may be magnified when the cloud provider has reserved the right to change its terms and policies at will. The secondary use of a Cloud computing user's information by the cloud provider may violate laws under which the information was collected or are otherwise applicable to the original user. A cloud provider will also acquire transactional and relationship information that may itself be revealing or commercially valuable. For example, the sharing of information by two companies may signal a merger is under consideration. In some instances, only the provider's policy will limit use of that information. Many users are likely not aware of the details set out in the terms of service for cloud providers or of the consequences of sharing information with a cloud provider.

For some types of information and some categories of Cloud computing users, privacy and confidentiality rights, obligations, and status may change when a user discloses information to a cloud provider.

Procedural or substantive barriers may prevent or limit the disclosure of some records to third parties, including Cloud computing providers. For example, health record privacy laws may require a formal agreement before any sharing of records is lawful. Other privacy laws may flatly prohibit personal information sharing by some corporate or institutional users. Professional secrecy obligations, such as those imposed on lawyers, may not allow the sharing of client information. Sharing information with a cloud provider may undermine legally recognized evidentiary privileges. Records management and disposal laws may limit the ability of a government agency to use Cloud computing for official records.

Disclosure and remote storage may have adverse consequences for the legal status of or protections for personal or business information.

For example, a trade secret shared with a cloud provider may lose some of its legal protections. When a person stores information with a third party (including a Cloud computing provider), the information may have fewer or weaker privacy protections than when the information remains only in the possession of the person. Government agencies and private litigants may be able to obtain information from a third party more easily than from the original owner or creator of the content. A cloud provider might even be compelled to scan or search user records to look for fugitives, missing children, copyright violations, and other information of interest to government or private parties. In addition, remote storage may undermine security or audit requirements.

The location of information in the cloud may have significant effects on the privacy and confidentiality protections of information and on the privacy obligations of those who process or store the information.

Any information stored in the cloud eventually ends up on a physical machine owned by a particular company or person located in a specific country. That stored information may be subject to the laws of the country where the physical machine is located. For example, personal information that ends up maintained by a cloud provider in a European Union Member State could be subject permanently to European Union privacy laws.

Information in the cloud may have more than one legal location at the same time, with differing legal consequences.

A cloud provider may, without notice to a user, move the user's information from jurisdiction to jurisdiction, from provider to provider, or from machine to machine. The legal location of information placed in a cloud could be one or more places of business of the cloud provider, the location of the computer on which the information is stored, the location of a communication that transmits the information from user to provider and from provider to user, a location where the user has communicated or could communicate with the provider, and possibly other locations.

Laws could oblige a cloud provider to examine user records for evidence of criminal activity and other matters.

Some jurisdictions in the United States require computer technicians to report to police or prosecutors evidence of child pornography that they find when repairing or otherwise servicing computers. To the extent that Cloud computing places a diverse collection of user and business information in a single location, it may be tempting for governments to ask or require cloud providers to report on particular types of criminal or offensive behavior or to monitor activities of particular types of users (e.g., convicted sex offenders). Other possibilities include searching for missing children and for music or software copyright violations.

Legal uncertainties make it difficult to assess the status of information in the cloud as well as the privacy and confidentiality protections available to users.

The law badly trails technology, and the application of old law to new technology can be unpredictable. For example, current laws that protect electronic communications may or may not apply to Cloud computing communications or they may apply differently to different aspects of Cloud computing.

Responses to the privacy and confidentiality risks of Cloud computing include better policies and practices by cloud providers, changes to laws, and more vigilance by users.

If the Cloud computing industry would adopt better and clearer policies and practices, users would be better able to assess the privacy and confidentiality risks they face. Users might avoid Cloud computing for some classes of information and might be able to select a service that meets their privacy and confidentiality needs for other categories of information. For those risks that cannot be addressed by changes in policies and practices, changes in laws may be appropriate. Each user of a cloud provider should pay more – and indeed, close – attention to the consequences of using a cloud provider and, especially, to the provider's terms of service.

SIX: SOFTWARE AS A SERVICE, THE BUSINESS MODEL

In a SaaS business model, software applications are provided via the Internet, and a usage fee is paid on a subscription or per-use basis. This business model for software delivery is in contrast to the traditional in-house enterprise/business applications which have typically been supported, upgraded, and controlled by the in-house IT organization and are dependent on the expertise that resides within an organization. The consumer software business model of SaaS can be less expensive than the traditional model by reducing the IT infrastructure and costs associated with this overhead. Conversely, customers relinquish software version control and update requirements. In addition, costs to use the service become a continuous expense rather than a single expense at the time of purchase. SaaS revenue streams to the vendor are lower initially than traditional software license fees, but are also recurring, and thus viewed as more predictable, much like maintenance fees for licensed software. While SaaS is not entirely new (airline reservations, email programs, web conferencing systems are examples of existing SaaS hosted applications), this software business model has become a growing business, having been enabled through advancements in bandwidth, Web technologies, and Internet flexibility to interact with any computing operating platform. In a broader context, SaaS is one component of what is referred to as a "Cloud computing environment", where computing services are made available through a virtualized environment accessible through the Web. These virtualized products include application platforms, infrastructure, and SOA, in addition to software that is obtained remotely.

Enormous economies of scale can be achieved in the deployment, management and support of SaaS applications through a data and architectural design that is specifically built with a "multi-tenant" backend, thus allowing multiple customers to access a shared data model. While multi-tenancy requires an architecture that maximizes the sharing of resources, it still needs to be able to differentiate data belonging to different customers. Achieving economies of scale also relies on a model where multiple customers access a single version of an application. To meet varying customer needs, the application must be flexible enough to be customized based on customer needs.

In addition to being multi-tenant-efficient, a well-designed SaaS application needs to be configurable and scalable. Several key architectural models exist; the maturity of these models is distinguished by the addition of many attributes. The choice of architectural model depends on the needs of the business, including ease of implementation, number of users, information security requirements, type of application and cost.

SaaS Architecture

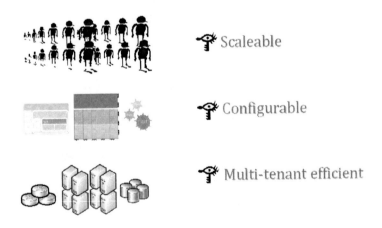

Figure 4: Notional SaaS Architecture SaaS Benefit Analysis

Sound reasons exist for businesses to consider the SaaS business model as an alternative to traditional delivery models of IT. These benefits include:

- *Users pay for "needed" functionality.* In the SaaS business model, the user pays for what is used, rather than technology that is not needed or used.

- *SaaS is treated as an operating expense.* This allows departments to keep within their budget authority.

- *SaaS offers a lower total cost of ownership alternative.* This can be achieved through a less expensive implementation model, where on-site installation of underlying infrastructure is not needed, and SaaS service configuration is administered via the browser. With the management of the operational aspects of running the application and supporting infrastructure passed on to the provider, IT management offloads this responsibility, allowing it to focus on higher value-added, more mission-critical tasks. Moreover, SaaS solutions are typically based on a low price/performance commercial proposition, and avoid a future spike in expenses that occur from on-premise upgrades that can be as much as 30% of the initial deployment costs. Finally, switching SaaS vendors is not nearly as significant as with on-premise solutions, making for a more effective buyer-supplier relationship in the ensuing years.

- *Business expansion is enabled with a SaaS model.* Since application usage and processing are done from a virtual, hosted location accessed through a web browser, users from diverse, remote locations can access the application. This flexibility allows organizations to experience business growth, including expansion to diverse locations, without experiencing the large costs associated with such expansion. This growth potential leads to the possibility of the SaaS business approach being disruptive in nature to software application providers. The accessibility of applications through the Internet has the potential to accelerate its adoption to billions of users.

- *The vendor is responsible for delivering effective applications.* Vendors control version releases and have the latest updates and patches, relieving the subscriber of the software maintenance, complexity of operation and support, and high initial investment costs. Secondary, indirect benefits arise from adoption of the delivery model, including relieving recruiting and retention pressures, costs, and continuity of service of IT resources in high demand.

POTENTIAL RISKS

Consideration of risks is important in decisions to migrate to SaaS as a consumer. Some of these issues include:

- *Perception of heightened data vulnerability exists with the adoption of a SaaS model.* Moving to the virtualized world of SaaS would imply a greater exposure to potential external threats to data security. However, most mature SaaS suppliers have security levels equal to the typical enterprise IT environment. In addition, clarity must be achieved on who is responsible for the management and control of the data.

- *SaaS may offer only basic functionality.* SaaS can, in some cases, be too simple and basic to fulfill user requirements, as these needs expand and develop. This lack of customization of applications can create a real struggle to support more complex processes in more mission-critical business activities. The culture of customization prevalent in on-premise applications is not readily accepted in SaaS environments because of the high-volume, relatively low-transaction-value business model.

- *Lack of availability of the Internet creates application inaccessibility.* Reliance on the Internet is the fundamental underpinning of the SaaS model, and hence this solution is vulnerable to Internet instabilities.

- *Integration of the application with other supporting applications and/or infrastructure can be pushed to the customer.* In the still-fledgling world of SaaS, consumers cannot take for granted the role that the vendor will play in integration in this still "learn-as-you-go" phase for both vendors and customers of the SaaS model. The back-end system integration points selected will be a major factor in gaining true productivity from an outsourced SaaS application.

Risks to the SaaS business model also exist for the provider, particularly those that provide through a subscription cost model. Customers may consume more than the provider anticipated. In general, enterprise software companies face a formidable challenge in making the strategic shift from entire revenue models based on a traditional license stream to a smaller – albeit more regular – influx of monthly revenue.

Seven: SaaS and Business Performance

SaaS is generally associated with business software and is typically thought of as a low-cost way for businesses to obtain the same benefits of commercially licensed, internally operated software without the associated complexity and high initial cost. Many types of software are well suited to the SaaS model, where customers may have little interest or capability in software deployment, but do have substantial computing needs. There are numerous benefits to adopting and utilizing the SaaS model. Some of these include:

- Eliminating the need to install and run the application on the customer's own computer
- Alleviating the customer's burden of software maintenance, ongoing operation, and support
- Reducing the up-front expense of software purchases, through less costly, on demand pricing
- Providing stronger protection of intellectual property and establish an ongoing revenue stream

Alternately, there are a few points that may negatively affect SaaS adoption. Some of these points are:

- Lack of Customer control over software versions or changing requirements
- Business model where the service becomes a continuous expense, rather than a single expense at time of purchase

There are numerous applications for which SaaS should be considered to support businesses. They include:

- Customer Relationship Management (CRM)

- Videoconferencing
- Human Resources
- IT services management
- Accounting
- Web Analytics
- Web Content management
- E-Mail

SaaS applications are generally priced on a per-user basis, sometimes with a relatively small minimum number of users and often with additional fees for extra bandwidth and storage. SaaS revenue streams to the vendor are therefore lower initially than traditional software license fees, but are also recurring, and therefore viewed as more predictable, much like maintenance fees for licensed software.

CHALLENGES TO BUSINESS PERFORMANCE

There are several business challenges that must be examined and taken into consideration when adopting SaaS. A few of the most encountered business challenges include:

- Widespread implementation of SaaS requires that the services be well defined so that one can achieve an economy of scale and develop capacity to meet supply and recover cost. This need is especially true for those areas of IT that are ubiquitous, enterprise and commodity-like. SaaS is therefore not suitable for innovative or highly specialized niche systems, though SaaS may be used to provide one or more components in such systems.

- As with manufacturing, a lack of substitutability and second sourcing options with any commodity creates a strategic weakness for any customer in terms of security, competition and pricing. Various forms of this weakness, such as 'vendor lock-in', are often cited as a barrier to adoption of SaaS as the current industry lacks portability and interoperability between vendors. This means that to change from one vendor to another will take a considerable amount of effort and time. This situation is resolvable by the introduction of open source standards and the development of markets based upon such standards.

- Concerns over potential security and operational risk are usually countered with the argument that the professionals operating SaaS applications may have much better security and redundancy tools available to them.

- There is a concern that SaaS applications pose some difficulty for businesses that need extensive customization. It is usually countered with the claim that many vendors have made progress with both customization and publication of their programming interfaces. Also, it should be noted that customization will reduce substitutability and, given that SaaS covers commodity-like activities, the strategic benefit of customization is highly dubious.

THREE MAJOR SAAS BUSINESS CONSIDERATIONS

As enterprise end-users increasingly look to on-demand software as a key time and money saver, the burden of delivering SaaS falls squarely on the shoulders of the software vendor. New non-strategic hosting requirements and revenue model shifts constitute a huge addition to core competency of building and selling competitive enterprise software. Providing SaaS requires functionality such as virtualization, multi-tenancy, data partitioning, usage metering, contract and subscriptions management, service provisioning, hosting infrastructure, security, revenue collection, and more. These requirements introduce technological and business challenges that business leaders will need to explore and consider in the evolving software as a service business model. There is no doubt; enterprise software users want application on-demand. Changing the traditional on-premise software business model to a SaaS software business model will involve the following business challenges:

1. Leasing versus Owning

A true SaaS business model will involve shifting the ownership of the software to an external provider. Business leaders traditionally purchase the rights to use various software applications through licensing. This new concept of SaaS versus traditional ownership of software through licensing will represent a significant change in the traditional business model and subsequent business decisions.

Much like leasing or buying a car, there are many different factors to consider when deciding whether to lease software through a SaaS vendor or own the software through the traditional software provider. When an enterprise leases software, it does not own the rights to the software. A SaaS vendor will retain the rights to the software and "rents" it over a specified period of time. In the traditional software business model, business leaders only purchase the right to use a copy of the software. For all practical purposes, it is as though the company "owns" the software and may use it as often, and for as long as it likes.

Up-front costs for software as a product usually include the cash price, taxes, and software registration. Under a SaaS business model there is a monthly software lease payments because businesses will be paying only for the software's depreciation during the software lease term, plus rent charges which may include interest, taxes, and fees. In addition, much like leasing a car, companies may be responsible for early termination charges should they decide to terminate the lease early. However, one advantage to the SaaS model may be that developers and software architects have the advantage of using the most technologically advanced "bleeding edge" software every 1-2 years or sooner. Many customers are eager for the shift because they are frustrated by the traditional cycle of buying a software license, paying for a service contract and then having to buy upgrades. Many customers believe they would have more control over the relationship if they simply paid monthly fees that could be switched to another vendor if the first failed to perform.

By owning the software outright, companies pay for a subscription to software running on someone else's servers – software that goes away when they stop subscribing. At the end of the lease period they "walk away". Others have argued that SaaS solutions cost more over time because customers continue to pay subscription fees throughout the lifetime of the application. However some researchers suggest that competition will render the traditional licensed model unsustainable in some application categories: Ownership costs are typically less — as much as 30% lower for a typical CRM installation, according to McKinsey & Co analysis. Costs should drop even faster for commodity services such as e-mail and messaging, which may soon be offered at prices so low that the traditional licensing model will be uneconomical. Therefore in reviewing the benefits of the traditional software as a product versus a SaaS business model, it will be especially important to understand how SaaS may provide a more direct and quantifiable economic benefit over the traditional on-premise software business model.

2. Responsibility for technology infrastructure and management

Supporting SaaS will require finding talented software developers and architects and letting them loose on projects. Research suggests that a SaaS business model will require a certain type of iterative thinking, and multitasking ability that typical software developers and architects may not possess. That is, the most qualified prospects on paper may not necessarily be capable of grasping the nuances of SaaS, or might be stuck in the old software delivery model.

Research further suggests that in a typical IT environment based around on-premise software, the majority of the budget is spent on hardware and professional services – leaving a minority of the budget available for software. In terms of hardware, there is the potential for cost savings by converting to a true SaaS business model. The majority of the typical IT budgets are allocated on hardware, (i.e., desktop computers, servers, networking components, and mobile devices that provide users access to the software) and professional services resources. In a true SaaS business model, transferring the IT responsibilities to a SaaS provider should result in significant cost savings. Hardware costs will be significantly reduced as the SaaS vendor will host the software applications. Likewise, the professional services (i.e., the people and support staff required to deploy and maintain the hardware and software environment, and ensure the continued operation and availability of the system, including technical support staff, etc.) traditionally required to support an on-premise software environment will also be minimized, thereby resulting in significant potential cost savings. True SaaS business models relieve the customer organization from the responsibility of supporting the hosted software, and purchasing and maintaining server hardware to host on-premise applications. This could potentially free-up dollars to invest in other business areas such as customization and development to support other in-house applications and more frequent equipment refresh to the desktop.

3. Leveraging Economy of Scale

The architectural foundations for a SaaS application will inevitably encounter the age-old build versus buy decision. SaaS enablement is hot right now, giving vendors a plethora of options on the buy side. Many leading thinkers on information technology support the buy scenario, and specifically urge vendors to buy into horizontally aligned SaaS platforms serving multiple vendor-instigated verticals because of issues arising with subscriber usage and economies of scale. An example some point to is Intuit's TurboTax online, where the service from this system ground to a snail's pace because of the mad rush of Americans filing taxes earlier in the year. A similar example might be the usage peaks that an accounting application might experience at the end of each quarter as sales are tied up at a frenzied pace by using some form of SaaS accounting product. SaaS vendors will need to provide and ensure high availability of service even during unusual high peak times. Therefore in most cases, aggregation of resources will lead to economies of scale.

SaaS platforms will provide that aggregation, normalizing the usage spikes across many vertically aligned vendor applications. The primary way to do this is by sharing the resources with other companies that also need high availability service but whose peak times are different. SaaS platforms will be able to achieve these economies of scale through mass aggregation of requirements and management of resources. Some SaaS platform providers such as Apex and SaaSGrid which aggregate infrastructure requirements are taking the solution a step further by providing guarantees of service at any point in time without software providers explicitly having to build out an infrastructure or request a larger slice of the computing pie during high volume times. By eliminating much of the upkeep, and using the economics of scale to combine and centralize customers' hardware and services requirements, the research suggests that SaaS vendors can offer solutions at a much lower cost than traditional vendors, not only in monetary terms, but also by greatly reducing the need for customers to add complexity to their IT infrastructure.

Eight: SaaS Cost Benefit Analysis

There are many arguments that can be made in favor of SaaS applications. In particular, there are four key elements of the cost benefit analysis that make a surprising but resounding case for deploying SaaS applications. These four elements are:

1. Making the IT budget go further

2. Better estimation of people services

3. Better growth management

4. Accountability of the SaaS vendor

Making the IT Budget Go Further

The first element in the cost benefit analysis of SaaS applications is that SaaS provides a direct and quantifiable economic benefit over the traditional software model.

In a typical organization, the IT budget is spent in three broad areas:

- Software - The programs and data that the organization utilizes for computing and information processing.

- Hardware - The desktop computers, servers, networking components and mobile devices that provide users with access to the software.

- People Services - The people and institutions that ensure the continued operation and availability of the system, including internal support staff, professional services consultants and vendor representatives.

Figure 5: Typical cost for on-premise environment

Of these three, it is the software that is most directly involved in information management, which is the ultimate goal of any IT organization. Hardware and people services, though vital and important components of the IT environment, are properly considered means to an end, in that they make it possible for the software to produce the desired end result of effective information management. (To put it another way, any organization would gladly add software functionality without extra hardware if it could do so effectively, but no organization would simply add hardware without an anticipated need to add software as well.) In an IT environment based around premise-based software, the majority of the budget is typically spent on hardware and people services, leaving a minority of the budget available for software. In this model, the software budget is spent primarily on licensed copies of "shrink-wrapped" business software and customized line-of-business software. The hardware budget is spent on desktop and mobile computers for end-users, servers to host data and applications, and components to network them together. The professional services budget pays for a support staff to deploy and support software and hardware, as well as consultants and development resources to help design and build custom systems.

Note: The proportions shown in these diagrams are for illustrative *purposes only; they are not intended to advocate any specific allocation of resources.*

In an organization relying chiefly on SaaS, the IT budget allocation looks much different. In this model, the SaaS vendor hosts critical applications and associated data on central servers at the vendor's location, and it supports the hardware and software with a dedicated support staff. This would relieve organizations from the responsibility of supporting the hosted software and for purchasing and maintaining server hardware for it. Moreover, applications delivered over the Web or through smart clients place significantly less demand on a desktop computer than

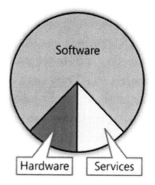

Figure 6: Typical budget for a SaaS environment

traditional locally-installed applications, which would extend the desktop technology lifecycle significantly. The end result is that a much larger percentage of the IT budget would be available to spend on software, typically in the form of subscription fees to SaaS providers.

Leveraging SaaS Economies of Scale

It is important to note that a percentage of the subscription fees paid to SaaS vendors for "software" pay for hardware and professional services for the vendor. A SaaS vendor with x number of customers subscribing to a single, centrally-hosted software service enables the vendor to serve all of its customers in a consolidated environment. For example, a line-of-business SaaS application installed in a load balanced farm of five servers may be able to support 50 medium-sized customers. This means that each customer would only be responsible for a tenth of the cost of a server. A similar application installed locally might require each customer to dedicate an entire server to the application—perhaps more than one, if load balancing and high availability are concerns. This represents a substantial *potential* savings over the traditional model. For SaaS applications that are built to scale well, the operating cost for each customer will continue to drop as more customers are added. As this is happening, the provider will develop multi-tenancy as a core competency, *leading to higher-quality offerings at a lower cost.* Therefore, even accounting for the hardware and professional services costs incurred by SaaS vendors, companies can still obtain significantly greater pure software functionality for the same IT budget.

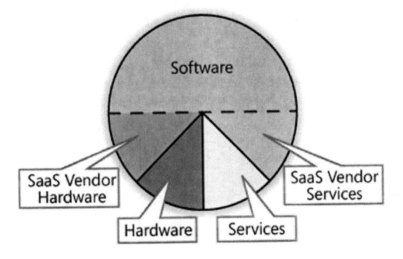

Figure 7: Typical budget for a SaaS model accounting for hardware and people cost

BETTER ESTIMATION OF PEOPLE SERVICES

The second key element in the cost benefit analysis of SaaS applications is the underestimated people costs associated with running premise-based traditional software applications. Calculating the real cost of people services is not easy and as a result is sometimes omitted from the TCO (Total Cost of Ownership) analysis. This can lead to an "apples to oranges" comparison. To quote a prospect from one SaaS vendor: "We do not know how to estimate our people services, so we choose not to consider them when comparing the cost of WebEx vs. the premise-based software alternative". The META Group, a consulting company, determined that "in today's economic environment, even minimal cost savings per seat are tantamount to freeing up discretionary IT investment dollars that might be applied in the enterprise technology portfolio or elsewhere in the organization. Companies no longer have the luxury of looking solely at hardware and software procurement costs and run rates of their technology investments but must examine the purchase decisions across their life cycle as well as how their people are spending their time servicing the application. While companies understand and scrutinize the cost of software and hardware very well, personnel costs are usually not examined as closely as they should be. Examining all these cost factors as a whole and how they impact is paramount in running an efficient organization."

Personnel Costs Can Be as High as 75%
Gartner Inc, a global analyst firm tracking the high tech market estimates "that more than 75% of the IT budget is spent just maintaining and running existing systems and software infrastructure". In addition, Gartner believes that "customers can spend up to four times the cost of their software license per year to own and manage their applications". Another data point comes from Microsoft, which in 2002 told the Wall Street Journal: "that the initial purchase is usually only 5% of the total

cost of owning and maintaining a program". IDC, another global analyst firm, came to a similar conclusion when it did an analysis of the web conferencing industry. It determined that "hidden personnel costs can be as high as 70% of the total cost to run premise-based conferencing software".

Companies seem to instinctively understand this as most have outsourced their audio conferencing applications to audio conferencing vendors. Since running audio bridges is not a core business for most companies, they consider outsourcing these applications to audio conferencing vendors like AT&T, Verizon, Intercall and BT.

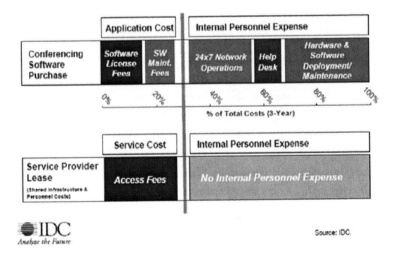

Figure 8: Personnel Expense Comparison (IDC)

E-mail and Groupware Applications Costs Support This Analysis

By virtue of the extensive experience that enterprises have with e-mail and groupware, the economics of these services are well understood. Analyst reports show that "the personnel costs for these traditional software applications are at a minimum 2.5 times, and can be as much as 7.5 times, the software costs (including maintenance), with a typical range of personnel expenses being 5 to 7 times the software and maintenance costs over a 3-year period".

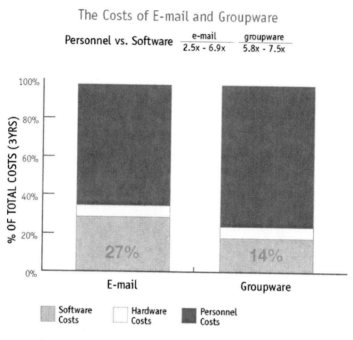

The Costs of E-mail and Groupware

Figure 9: Personnel cost are the largest part of TCO for email and groupware

SAAS ALLOWS BETTER GROWTH MANAGEMENT

The third key element in the cost benefit analysis is that SaaS applications grow with the business. Companies do not have to make decisions on the type of application they need restricted by their own size, but instead they can make decisions based solely on their business needs. Because of the economies of scale offered by the multi-tenant architecture, SaaS vendors can provide enterprise grade applications in any number of user levels. For arguments sake, let's use the "named user" licensing model to explain this. A named user license model means that a specific end-user has the right to use the application. For example; if a company has 100 employees that need access to a specific application, they would buy 100 named user licenses. The company does not have a need to roll out the application to all 100 employees at the same time. With a traditional software model, the company would need to deploy hardware infrastructure to support the application and train its IT staff to install, maintain and troubleshoot the application. In most cases it does not make sense to do this to support only five or ten employees. As a result, the company may buy all 100 licenses up front.

In the case of the SaaS application, there is no hardware infrastructure to acquire or IT staff to train. This means that the company can start by purchasing just five or ten licenses, and buy additional licenses as the need grows. This is especially important when budgets and resources are tight. As a result, the SaaS application is much friendlier to a growth model when compared to the traditional software application.

There is another important use-case for this flexibility. Companies that are going through mergers and acquisitions many times have a very hard time aligning their back-end IT infrastructure. It can take many months for hardware to be deployed and networks to be built before users in a new location have access to all the services used in all other locations. This problem is much smaller for SaaS applications, since all that is necessary is an Internet connection, browser, and username and password to start using the application.

ACCOUNTABILITY OF THE SAAS VENDOR

The fourth key element in the cost benefit analysis is that SaaS vendors have greater accountability because of the subscription-based pricing model. SaaS customers can actually exert more control over their vendors than traditional software customers. SaaS customers pay a recurring subscription fee for the duration of the contract term. SaaS vendors are typically held to monthly service level agreements (SLA) and are financially motivated to maintain adequate support and operational requirements on a recurring basis. Traditional software vendors are paid a big upfront license fee in exchange for a perpetual license. They have few obligations after the software has been deployed. As a result, there is much more accountability from a SaaS vendor than from a traditional software vendor. If the SaaS service does not function properly, customers, by the simple act of withholding their payment and enforcing their SLAs, can exert much greater pressure on the SaaS vendor to provide a fix for the application than on a traditional software vendor.

Cost Benefit Analysis
What are the cost drivers for completing a TCO analysis?

- Capital Expenses
- Design and Deployment Costs
- On-going Infrastructure Costs
- On-going Operations, Training and Support Costs
- Miscellaneous Cost

Capital Expenses
Software and hardware, network infrastructure enhancements, monitoring and testing tools, security products, supplies, facilities and other required infrastructure are part of the typical capital acquisition expenditure. In many cases, upgrades to other infrastructure may be required for enhanced or additional

capability, which adds additional capital expense. This capital expense is an up-front cash outlay.

With SaaS, there are no perpetual software licenses to buy. The nature of SaaS is that *you pay for what you use*. Most SaaS models have a recurring cost structure. Businesses pay a monthly or annual service fee for as long as they use the service. This service fee typically includes maintenance, support, training and upgrades and is inclusive of all hardware, networking, storage, database, administration and other costs associated with SaaS delivery.

Design and Deployment Costs

Staff and contract labor needed to research, design, integrate, test, tune and launch is a significant cost associated with deploying an in-house solution. Server and network capabilities must be reassessed and augmented. End-user computer hardware, operating systems and applications have to be evaluated for compatibility with the selected server product and upgraded if necessary. System testing and tuning are necessary to ensure performance is acceptable for launch. Training for end-users and IT staff will be required. Launch activities, awareness and pilots all require IT resources.

Most SaaS applications can be deployed and put into production much faster and for a fraction of the cost compared to a traditional software solution. This is very important when the opportunity costs of getting the application deployed are high. On the flip side, because a SaaS application is a multi-tenant application, there are less ways to customize the application to fit the business process.

Ongoing Infrastructure Costs

For ongoing operation, network monitoring and management tools are often required to enable real-time problem diagnosis and responsiveness. Additional networking equipment and bandwidth may be needed to accommodate incremental traffic that cannot be efficiently managed on the internal network. Yearly software maintenance and support contracts and system upgrades make a large contribution to the total cost of ownership. Capacity increases, multiple redundant systems, and add-on feature sets further increase cost. Hardware repair and replacement and recurring environmental costs, such as specialized high-availability facilities and power consumption, add further to the ongoing cost. While these expenditures are spread out over the lifetime of the service, they must be considered in a full TCO analysis.

Other than additional Internet bandwidth needs, there are almost no incremental infrastructure costs to handle the growth of a SaaS application. This alone could represent a *significant costs savings*. Depending on the SaaS application, the IT organization may also have to deploy a desktop application to allow the end-user to communicate with the application. Finally some API (Application Programmable Interface) development may be required to configure the application to better integrate with existing Enterprise Applications. Scaling the infrastructure and the costs associated with growth are fully the responsibility of the SaaS provider.

Ongoing Operations, Training and Support Costs

IT organizations will have to allocate resources for monitoring, supporting and maintaining the application. If the application is new, the IT organization will have to train and certify existing personnel and/or recruit new personnel with or without pre-existing application certification. The IT organization will also be responsible for monitoring and maintaining the application and troubleshooting the application in case of downtime. In addition, every time a patch or upgrade needs to be deployed, additional IT resources will be required. This is typically the biggest hidden cost that needs to be considered when making the buying decision for a new application. If this cost is incorrectly estimated, any affect on revenue or cost reduction can greatly change.

Initial and ongoing training is another success factor for the broad adoption of a new application. A vendor may offer initial training or a train–the-trainer session as part of the upfront cost, but with most traditional software applications, it is an internal department that is tasked with the initial and ongoing end-user training. Again, incorrect estimates can greatly affect expected revenue or cost reduction.

Support is the final and most critical success factor to the successful adoption and ongoing use of a new application. Whenever end-users have problems with the application, this can lead to a loss in productivity or in the worst case a refusal to use the application all together. This is also known as software turning into shelf ware. User issues typically grow with usage and, as such, the support load in the IT organization grows as well. If you add external use of the application to this equation, support issues and the costs associated with this typically grow exponentially. Again, if this cost is wrongly estimated, any affect on revenue or cost reduction can greatly change.

SaaS vendors are responsible for the end-to-end delivery of the application. The only responsibility of the IT organization is to ensure that the necessary ports on the firewall are open and that there is enough Internet access capacity available to allow the end-user base to communicate with the application. SaaS is a recurring service, so for a SaaS vendor the sale does not end when the initial contract is signed. If the application is not used, they can simply choose not to renew the contract at the end of the contract term. This is called churn. A traditional software vendor does not have to worry about churn, since customers buy upfront perpetual user licenses. As a result, SaaS vendors have a vested interest in seeing customers widely adopt and use the application. It is for this reason that almost all SaaS vendors focus on making their products easy to use and offer initial and ongoing end-user training. This training is in most cases included in the service fees. Finally, SaaS vendors also offer 1st, 2nd and 3rd line of support to their customers. This is for the same reasons they offer ongoing training services: if customers churn because of training or support issues, it will have an immediate impact to the SaaS vendor's bottom line.

Miscellaneous Costs

While the intangible costs are harder to measure and therefore are more difficult to include in a TCO analysis, they are no less real. Some of the intangible cost factors that affect TCO include:

- Reliability and Availability: Failed interactions mean lost employee time and lost opportunities, and may require repeat efforts to persuade users to retry the technology with increasing resistance. What SLA does the SaaS vendor offer and how do they compare to the internal SLA the IT organization offers?

- Interoperability: How easy is it to integrate with other applications?

- Extensibility: How easy is it to customize the application to fit the needs of the organization?

- Security: The costs of a security breach can be catastrophic if confidential business information is stolen or made available to competitors. What are the security policies that are in place at the SaaS vendor and how do they compare to the internal policies? Many companies have very strict policies with regards to the distribution and storage of company sensitive and confidential information. As a result, they are wary of "handing over" the security and control of their data to SaaS vendors. For this reason, SaaS vendors have vigorous security and change control policies in place.

- Scalability: As user needs grow, the original system may not keep up. "Busy signals" or functional limitations consume employee time and mean lost opportunities. How well can the SaaS vendor accommodate growth and what are the costs associated with growing the internal application?

- Capacity: Usage and adoption within the enterprise is difficult to predict, making managing capacity difficult. The tradeoffs are poor performance on the one hand or underutilized infrastructure on the other. With SaaS this is more easily managed when compared to an internal application.

- Opportunity costs: The human resource and capital expenditures required by an in-house implementation come at the expense of other projects or could possibly delay the roll-out of new products and services, both of which have a direct impact on the bottom line.

One of the biggest TCO factors of premise-based traditional software applications is the cost of the ongoing people resources that are needed to monitor, maintain and upgrade the application and to provide training and support to the end-user base. These costs are not quoted as part of the cost of deploying the traditional software application and depending on the application, can be between 50 and 85% of the total cost of ownership for the application. Underestimating these costs can have a great impact on the overall TCO predication.

Big TCO factors associated with SaaS deployment are the subscription fees charged by the SaaS vendor. These fees cover the monitoring, maintenance and upgrades to the application as well as the training and support of the end-user base. Compared with the ongoing personnel costs of the traditional software application these costs are quoted as part of the cost of deploying the SaaS application.

Moving Away from "Owning" Software

With traditional software, the company buys a perpetual user license. This gives them the impression that they "own" the software and can use it at will and in perpetuity. With SaaS, instead of "owning" software, the company pays for a subscription to software running on the infrastructure owned by the SaaS provider. The company's right to use the software goes away once they stop paying for the subscription. They do not lose the rights and ownership of data stored on the infrastructure of the SaaS vendor.

The dynamic between subscription and ownership is used as a TCO argument in favor of buying traditional software. Why rent when you can buy, especially when the plan is to use the application for a long time. On the contrary, SaaS applications offer many advantages over traditional software including avoiding the huge hidden personnel cost in deploying, running and maintaining traditional software.

The Elusive Break-Even Point
Another argument for "owning" software has been that even with the higher upfront costs, there is a break-even point where traditional software becomes less expensive than the SaaS subscription model. The analyst firm IDC reviewed several SaaS versus traditional software deployments and found that when people resources and cost of upgrades are correctly taken in consideration, this break-even point may never be realized.

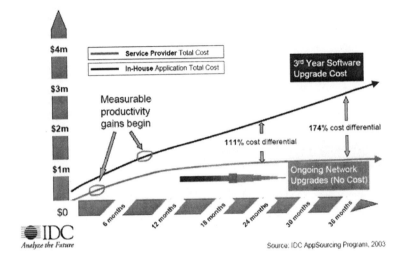

Figure 10: IDC's TCO Comparison

Nine: SaaS Technical Considerations and Architectural Options

There are several considerations to be made by an organization prior to using or providing SaaS applications. There are also important considerations to be made in comparing the traditional software development lifecycle to SaaS delivery model. Moreover, as a provider, SaaS applications can be developed and delivered in multiple architecture frameworks and models, which need to be examined and understood.

Technical Challenges

Even though SaaS is a software application developed using a traditional software development lifecycle, the technical challenges encountered in each of the lifecycle phases differ widely from the traditional software applications The five phases of the traditional software development lifecycle, depicted in Figure 11, comprise of Requirements, Architecture Design, Development, Testing & Integration, and Operations & Maintenance. The challenges for each are reviewed below.

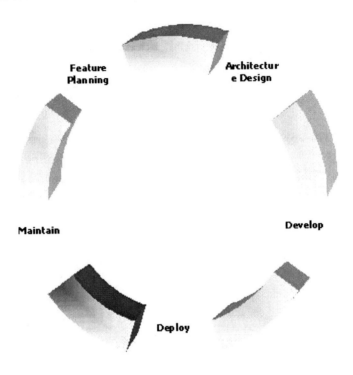

Figure 11: A Traditional Software Development lifecycle

Feature Planning - Requirements
Each customer will have unique business processes; therefore user requirements for each customer will change. These changes can vary from simple (e.g. logo, colors, fonts.) to complex (e.g. integrate customer's specific business rules within the application). Traditionally, customized "on-premise" software applications are developed to meet requirements for each customer. Each application has generally one customer and a specific set of software requirements from that customer. Conversely, in the SaaS model, a single application version is accessed by multiple customers; this provides economies of scale – one of the advantages of being a SaaS application provider. Therefore, when developing a SaaS application, the challenge is to maintain

flexibility such that the application can be customized to meet each client's unique business requirements without developing a new application or different versions for each customer. In the SaaS model, where many customers are utilizing one application version, the organizations construct changes. Business managers no longer have direct control of the software development or features being developed; they would therefore rely on a single application version to meet their specific needs.

Architecture and Design
Unlike traditional software applica application architectures have to be considered prior to being designed. These various architecture types – multi-tenant/multi-version, shared execution, managed hosting service, isolated tenancy, and multi-tenant / single-version – are discussed in detail below. In addition to these architecture types, scalability, database configuration and security must also be considered.

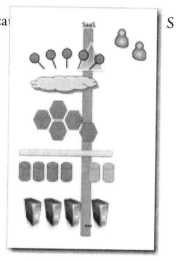

Figure 12: Scalable Architecture

Business customers will expect that the SaaS application providers' IT systems scale in an unlimited manner. Since multiple customers use the same application, each of these customers might add additional users simultaneously. The SaaS provider has to therefore be capable of addressing this "potential" real-time growth both in its hardware and in software. Database configuration and design are important factors in delivery of a successful SaaS application. In most SaaS applications (i.e. multi-tenant/single-version), a single database will serve more than one enterprise organization. This is unlike traditional software applications, in which only one client would use one database. The software architecture within a SaaS application has to be designed in such a manner that one database is able to support multiple customers and can be customized for each of these customers. Conversely, if a company is a user of SaaS, it has to verify that the provider is capable of scalability in its infrastructure and versatility in its software architecture. In terms of security, issues such as authentication, authorization, data isolation, and others arising from multi-tenancy are very significant in the SaaS model and issues that the hosting company has to deal with. Even though the database is shared across the clients, the application must be capable of keeping the data secure and not viewable by users from other clients.

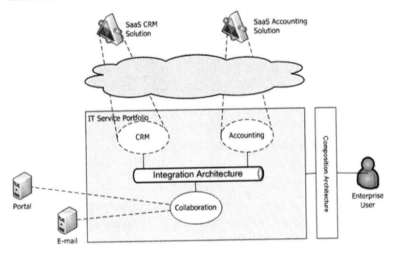

Figure 13: SaaS Deployment Architecture

The SaaS provider will want to keep unauthorized people from accessing the software. In addition, the SaaS application has to have the ability to protect each client's data. Companies could leverage expertise in the area of cyber security to better design databases and applications such that issues are not viewed as obstacles for our customers. SaaS applications typically use the Internet for delivery. The applications are going to be designed with that as a foremost requirement. This is an area where some companies would have to either re-train or hire new architects who are versed in developing applications with this model. The architecture and design phase is similar to a traditional software lifecycle development model; however the approach to the design is completely different. Security is a higher priority than on-premise application sitting behind a corporate firewall.

Development

SaaS is fast gaining momentum with traditional software development companies like Microsoft, Google, and Oracle all who have developed web based software products that are being offered to users as services. SaaS products require a different development approach than traditional software development. Traditional "plan-driven" development approaches does not work in a SaaS environment. Agility and timeliness are critical for rapid releases and upgrades. In today's world, getting the applications developed in the shortest time and getting them off-the-shelf for beta testing is the most acceptable approach. This provides an opportunity to absorb rapid and immediate customer feedback, leveraging usage data, and meeting customer expectations quickly. Agile development methodology approach seems to be gaining momentum for SaaS development. This approach is quite different than the waterfall model. Traditionally, enterprise software development companies have had difficulty to move to a SaaS model. Some of the challenges of a SaaS model include customer retention and service, continuing to operate in dual operational mode, and technical skills. However, similar to Microsoft, Google, and Oracle, the new development approach requires different development skills and capabilities therefore can be difficult for traditional enterprise software development companies. For developers, it means embracing new programming languages and working with open Web standards when creating enterprise level software. SaaS applications are built with end-user experience being the driving factor. Many companies already have developers capable of programming in Java, .Net, J2EE, etc., therefore the transition should not be difficult. These companies are hiring engineers with this end-user experience mindset already engrained because of consumer applications such as Facebook, MySpace, etc. In addition to development, there will be more of an emphasis on integration in the back-end support.

Testing and Integration
Testing and Integration of SaaS applications are similar to traditional software, with a twist. While functionality testing would not change much from traditional software testing, liability testing on the hand would have to be tested much more thoroughly than traditional software. After testing, integration is still needed and much more an effort would be required than traditional software testing. Both points are discussed in detail below. In the case of SaaS applications, the provider or user does not control the delivery infrastructure (Internet). The developer must measure the ability of the application to function under heavy load or degraded / slower connections. The scalability of the applications must also be measured. In the multi-tenancy applications, the hardware and software should be able to scale quickly and reliably over public domains (Internet). Unlike traditional software testing, this would require hosting infrastructure to test SaaS applications, which brings the cost of reliability testing higher than traditional software testing. Even though SaaS should bring economies of scale to the SaaS provider, each integration effort for each customer is going to be unique. The integration of the application has to be with an external endpoint through the Internet. The biggest Achilles heel being that each enterprise has a different configuration for firewalls, authorization and authentication. Additionally, each customer will have independent applications that need to be integrated with the SaaS application e.g. SQL based;

Oracle based, or internally developed – different APIs for HR or financial applications. As a SaaS development organization, a larger portion of time or money will be needed for testing and integration compared with traditional software. Lack of reliability testing would affect multiple customers simultaneously, since applications support multiple customers. Because of this, early and more frequent testing is required with SaaS applications versus traditional software development cycles. If the SaaS development organization already has a large system integration experience, smooth integration efforts could be a key differentiator in the marketplace.

Operations and Maintenance (O&M)

Deploying and maintaining a SaaS application forms another set of challenges that must be addressed. In "on-premise" software, the customer handles the deployment and maintenance of the software application once purchased, whereas a SaaS hosting provider generally deploys and maintains the application. Most companies in the traditional software-license business model do not have strong skills or expertise in network components or creating networks. Without this expertise, provisioning issues arise during initial infrastructure build out for new customers or during the reuse of equipment when a customer is upgraded or lost. After the initial provisioning, it is the responsibility of the hosting provider to maintain the hardware and the software for the application. Providers must be able to respond to service failures within an acceptable period. Generally, SaaS application providers will have an SLA with each customer. Most "On-Premise" software development companies do not have business or technical skills in-house to address these issues, but have an attitude of "fix it as fast as you can". This strategy might not work if multiple customers have simultaneous outages, in which one customer has a higher precedent SLA than do others. Furthermore, since the SaaS provider stores the customer data, the organization will need to have a formal disaster recovery plan should a catastrophic event affect the hosting site.

ARCHITECTURAL OPTIONS

SaaS can be used and delivered in multiple ways. There are advantages and disadvantages associated with the use of each of the architecture models that SaaS offers. Each organization should decide on the appropriate architecture that best fits the needs of the business. The table below outlines the five architectural models related to the application execution infrastructure: application versioning and data separation.

	Isolated Tenancy	Multi-Tenant Single Version	Multi-Tenant Multi-Version	Shared Execution	Managed Hosting Service
Application Execution Infrastructure	Dedicated	Shared	Shared	Shared	Dedicated
Application Versioning	Single	Single	Multiple	Single	Multiple
Data Separation	Physical	Logical	Logical or Physical	Physical	Physical

Figure 14: Architecture Options

Isolated Tenancy SaaS Model

An isolated tenancy model simply means that the application infrastructure is on a separate server that is dedicated to a single client. In this model, the database is physically separated and there is only one version of the application. Figure 15 illustrates the isolated tenancy model.

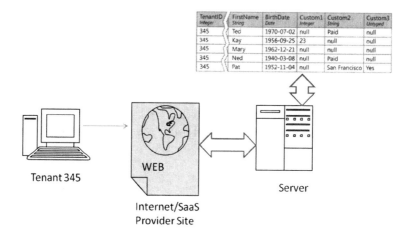

TenantID Integer	FirstName String	BirthDate Date	Custom1 Integer	Custom2 String	Custom3 Untyped
345	Ted	1970-07-02	null	Paid	null
345	Kay	1956-09-25	23	null	null
345	Mary	1962-12-21	null	null	null
345	Ned	1940-03-08	null	Paid	null
345	Pat	1952-11-04	null	San Francisco	Yes

Tenant 345

WEB

Internet/SaaS
Provider Site

Server

Figure 15: Isolated Tenancy Model

Some of the advantages of an isolated tenancy model include:

- No limitations to customization
- Greater access to information (e.g. query tools, report writers, and integration tolls)
- Multiple version control
- Mitigates peak period brown outs
- No interference from activities of other clients on the system
- Greater information security and privacy
- Restoring data from backups in the event of a failure is relatively simple
- Simple to implement
- Current IT staff can build off existing skills and knowledge of traditional software development
- Simplest architectural model to build

Some of the disadvantages of an isolated tenancy model include:

- More costly than multi-tenancy deployments
- Additional risk with system administration
- Limited deployment; very few isolated-tenancy applications are available
- Increased complexity when coordinating the roll out of new software releases
- Infrastructure costs are higher as only a limited number of databases can be supported on each server
- Hardware intensive

The isolated tenancy model is best suited for customers who are willing to pay for added security and privacy. It is also the most appropriate architectural model for high transactional applications such as financials.

Multi-Tenant/Single-Version SaaS Model

A multi-tenant/single-version model provides SaaS in an infrastructure that is shared by multiple clients. Only one version of the software is available at a given time, and each client's database is logically separated, but not physically separated from the others. Figure 16 illustrates the multi-tenant/single-version model.

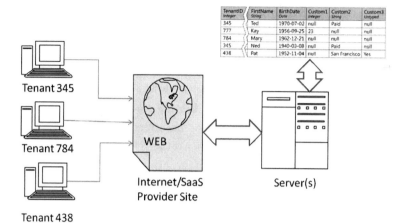

Figure 16: Multi Tenant/Single Version Model

Some of the advantages of a multi-tenant/single-version model include:

- Most economical of all architectural models to deliver
- Bug fixes can be addressed quickly
- Less hardware costs in the long term since many customers are using the same servers

Some of the disadvantages of a multi-tenant/single-version model include:

- Difficult to find IT staff with the skill-set for designing single-instance, multi-tenant architectures
- More difficult to implement than other SaaS models
- Vulnerable to risk due to single point of failure
- Security is a risk due to logical data separation
- Application upgrades are on the vendor's schedule, not the client's schedule
- Availability, flexibility, and scalability are downfalls

- Migrating to in-house implementation is not possible with this model

This model is most appropriate for less complex applications, such as commodity applications or tools, where there are fewer integration and data feed points. It lacks scalability and flexibility and is less likely to incorporate customer-specific features that enhance performance. In a multi tenant/single-version model, the advantages are mainly on the vendor's and not the client's side.

Multi-Tenant/Multi-Version SaaS Model

The Multi-Tenant/Multi-Version architectural model is an extension of the Multi-Tenant/Single-Version model, offering multiple versions of applications and/or services and may have shared or physically separate data instances. The service delivery infrastructure is designed to support multiple customers and optimized for the type of services/applications being provided. Figure 17 illustrates a multi-tenant/multi-version model.

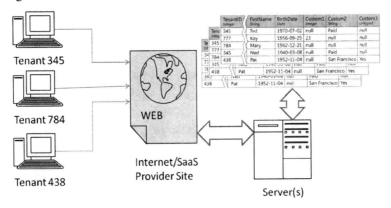

Figure 17: Multi Tenant/Multi Version Model

Because multiple customers are supported, little if any customization is available. Application and/or service design is driven largely by industry "best practices" and application popularity. Data from individual customers may be physically centralized but logically separated. The key difference between the Multi-Tenant models is the availability of multiple versions of the applications and/or services being offered. Customers can subscribe to one or several applications, and one or more versions of the same application. This allows the customer to upgrade application versions at their own pace rather than having an untimely or unneeded upgrade imposed on them as one of many tenants. It also may maintain the ability to use legacy data and execute a controlled transition to newer formats. A simple example would be to have the 2000, 2003 and 2007 versions of Microsoft Office available to the tenant. Infrastructure adequacy and version deployment are not issues because of the SaaS model and cutover to the newer version can be done at whatever pace is most effective for the tenant organization. The SaaS provider accomplishes maintenance and upgrade support for multiple application versions. Flow-down costs to tenant users are shared by all tenants, reducing the upkeep burden.

Some of the advantages of a multi-tenant/single-version model include:

- Since there are potentially many tenants sharing the same application delivery infrastructure and the database scheme, they are also sharing the costs, making for a lower per-tenant cost share. The flexibility of multiple application version availability allows tenants more control of cutover to newer versions. When data is logically separated, the privacy risks are potentially greater than with physical separation.

Some of the disadvantages of a multi-tenant/single-version model include:

- The cost of subscribing to/using several application versions is potentially higher than using a single version. Access by multiple users (tenants) can affect system/delivery performance due to the shared infrastructure of the SaaS provider. Should data security require a physically separate database, the cost of establishing and maintaining a separate database schema may be greater than logical separation but improves data privacy.

- This SaaS model facilitates tenant use of services/applications provided with only general infrastructure requirements on the tenant side. Tenants are responsible for establishing and maintaining their own Internet access, and individual user computers/workstations must be configured for optimum use of the desired applications/services (CPU, Memory, Video). Actual deployment of applications is done as quickly as the SaaS provider can create user accounts and authentications

- Tenants may need to obtain training on the applications/services available from the SaaS vendor or those providing the applications to the vendor.

Shared Execution Model

In the Shared-Execution model, delivery infrastructure and application execution are shared between all clients, using a single application version with physically separated database instances for each client. Because the application version and delivery structure are shared, all costs associated with those aspects are also shared. Figure 18 illustrates a shared execution architectural option.

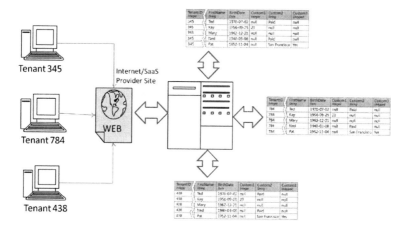

Figure 18: Shared Execution Model

The physically separated databases improve data privacy but could potentially incur greater upkeep costs per client than a shared-instance schema. However, if data security/privacy is a primary consideration, then this cost might not be an issue. The SaaS vendor, not the client, controls application customization and updating/upgrading. Performance may be impacted as all users share the same delivery infrastructure and application. Clients whose businesses require a high volume of activity with their database might want to consider one of the other SaaS models.

Some of the advantages of a multi-tenant/single-version model include:

- Potentially lower client costs due to shared application and delivery infrastructure.
- Physically separated databases enhance data privacy.

Some of the disadvantages of a multi-tenant/single-version model include:

- Physically separated databases may add cost.

87

- High transaction volume may negatively affect application performance since all clients are sharing both the application and delivery infrastructure.

The SaaS model facilitates tenant use of services/applications provided with only general infrastructure requirements on the client side. Clients are responsible for establishing and maintaining their own Internet access/bandwidth, and individual user computers/workstations must be configured for optimum use of the application/services (e.g. CPU, Memory, Video). Actual deployment of applications is done as quickly as the SaaS provider can create user accounts and authentications. Clients may need to obtain training on the applications/services available from the SaaS vendor or those providing the applications to the vendor.

Managed Hosting Service Model

Not strictly a SaaS model, the Managed Hosting Service model provides an infrastructure where all resources, hardware and software, are entirely dedicated to a single client. Any application can be supported, as well as multiple application versions. Because the hosted service is for a unique client, a high degree of application customization is possible. For the same reason, data security is potentially very high and the next best thing to keeping it in-house. Unfortunately, the same reasons that make this model attractive also make it potentially the most expensive way to outsource application hosting. The client covers operational fees and equipment amortization for the entire infrastructure. Figure 19 illustrates the Managed Hosting Service Model.

Some of the advantages of a managed hosting service model include:

- Highest level of data security and greatest potential for application flexibility, versioning, and customization.

• There is no performance issue related to multiple clients.

A disadvantage of a managed hosting service model is that it may potentially be the highest cost service option.

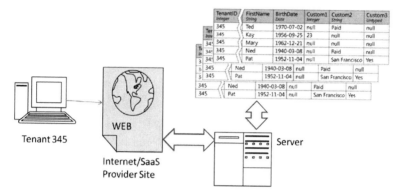

Figure 19: Managed Hosting Service Model

Ten: Impact of Virtualization

Virtualization is the one of highest impact issues changing infrastructure and operations through year 2012. It will change how you manage, how and what you buy, how you deploy, how you plan and how you charge. It will also shake up licensing, pricing and component management. Infrastructure is on an inevitable shift from components that are physically integrated by vendors (for example, monolithic servers) or manually integrated by users, to logically composed "fabrics" of computing, Input/Output (I/O) and storage components.

Server Infrastructure Virtualization
As virtualization matures, the "next big thing" will be automating the composition and management of the virtualized resources. Storage has already been virtualized, but primarily within the scope of individual vendor architectures. Networking has also been virtualized. The leading edge of this change is server virtualization. Roughly 90% of the server market is composed of x86 architecture servers. Based on a traditional model of one application per server, roughly 80% to 90% of the x86 computing capacity is unused at any one time. This unused capacity needs to be managed as it takes up data center space and requires power and cooling. Virtualization promises to unlock much of this underutilized capacity. IT organizations are approaching server virtualization as a cost-saving measure, and it is saving money. However, organizations that have a mature server virtualization deployment in place are leveraging virtualization for much more: faster deployments, reduced downtime, disaster recovery, variable usage accounting and usage chargeback, holistic capacity planning and more.

Virtualization of Client Computing

The key technology for defining new rules for device footprints is virtualization — a decoupling technology that breaks the close ties between hardware and software. A standard PC installation consists of a stack of multiple layers, the most important being hardware, the operating system and applications. Because of how these layers interact, the configuration of each is tightly coupled with the configuration of the layer below. This is the cause of much of the management complexity of today's PCs. Because hardware changes regularly, these changes have a geometric impact on everything above. Virtualization breaks these dependencies, so the installation of each layer is independent of the configuration of the layer below. On the PC, it occurs at two levels: between hardware and the OS (machine virtualization), and between the OS and applications (application virtualization). The impact of virtualization on the PC is the decoupling of the main functional layers. Application virtualization is gaining considerable interest, because key market changes are taking place. This type of virtualization is highly valuable for dealing with current PC management challenges, but it cannot help in the personal versus computing argument. Although more immediately accessible to you, its long-term impact will be far less significant than that of machine virtualization. This is the technology that will really make personal computing more manageable, flexible and secure by enabling users to define multiple isolated footprints on the same device.

Balancing Virtualization with Alternative Delivery Models
IT virtualization is the abstraction of IT resources in a way that masks the physical nature and boundaries of those resources from resource users. Virtualization can take place at various points in the IT architecture, and each point of virtualization creates an opportunity for alternative delivery models — new ways of delivering capability at that layer. Virtualization technologies will make it easy to consolidate to larger resources. However, virtualization technologies will also make distributed resources

easier to manage, re-provision and use efficiently. Several changes will make virtualization critical to most enterprises during the next few years. Processor capability has outpaced the performance requirements of many applications. Performance is relatively inexpensive and, therefore, the overhead of a virtualization layer is not an issue. Although processing power is inexpensive (and getting less expensive), space, power, installation, integration and administration are not, and they cost the same whether a resource is 10% or 90% utilized. Additionally, Web access has changed workload levels from relatively predictable to spiky, forcing enterprises to overprovision. Virtualization is not just about consolidation. By enabling alternative delivery models, new modes of providing functionality at each layer will evolve.

Virtualization Affects Software Models and Licensing
Virtualization technology breaks most established software pricing and licensing models. The concept of fractional use of large resources, the ability to quickly change the amount of capacity available to software, the ability to move software from one resource to another easily, and the concept of an offline snapshot (for recovery purposes, but still requiring updates and patches) are becoming more common. Finally, there is the idea that software could be packaged and delivered in a virtual machine (VM) format, ready to run, perhaps for a short period of time. None of these new concepts fit the common paradigm of pricing based on full use of a fixed asset. Virtualized licensing presents a major stumbling block to widespread adoption of virtualization. The industry has been slow to address the problem. As vendors change their software pricing and associated license provisions to accommodate virtual use, negotiators must plan to spend an increased amount of time per contract to understand the effect of such changes on their planned software use. Clients that do not diligently monitor the ways each of their vendors respond to virtual-use issues are likely to experience significant increased cost and the unintended impairment of their current license rights.

Operational and Management Impact of Virtualization
Server virtualization challenges many of the traditional tenets of
IT infrastructure, and this has ramifications on its management.
First is location. Most IT resources are fixed in their placement,
but virtual assets in many vendor implementations can move
dynamically. Second is how IT resources are represented — that
is, as files. This makes some activities, such as provisioning, easier
but may present a greater challenge in terms of security. Packaging
is changing as well. VMs are being packaged as "appliances." This
removes some of the volatility that might stem from configuration
variability, but the opaqueness of this approach raises issues about
what is "inside" the appliance packaging.
A key part of a virtual server initiative is the process of assessing
server and application candidates for virtualization. The goal is
not just to maximize density, but also to "right-size" workloads
through an understanding of application behavior. Most
enterprises attempt to place roughly similar types of workloads
on the same host or server because the effects of widely varying
demand could have deleterious effects on the overall quality of
service. This also means it is rare (but tempting) to co-mingle
low-use test VMs with more-consumptive production VMs
because the former environment is more dynamic, and the
constant powering on and off of VMs can be felt across the entire
server. It is important to enact a formalized assessment process
not only to predict application behavior, but also to let it run
for a while in production isolation as a preventive or insurance
measure. Initial placement, however, should not be an end to the
exercise — one goal should be continuous optimization. Overall
systems performance issues could be a sign of suboptimal VM
placement. Remember that no computing activity is free in terms
of its environmental costs. In addition, although the supporting
virtualization technology becomes increasingly capable in terms
of the types of applications it can support, conventional wisdom

still says that high I/O-based environments are better left running on real hardware — for now.

Security Considerations for Virtualization
Virtualization offers IT departments opportunities to reduce cost and increase agility; however, if this is done without implementing best practices for security, the resultant security incidents will increase costs and reduce agility. Security must be "baked in" from conception, not addressed later as an afterthought. The costs of implementing the best practices are significant and must be included in any analysis of the projected cost savings of virtualization. If these added security costs are avoided, the decision maker in the move to virtualize must accept the risk of not making the necessary security investments. The security considerations and best practices outlined in this Special Report should be utilized as a framework in the evaluation and selection of VM-aware security tools, and in the planning, building, operating, and managing of secure VM environments. Existing virtualization solutions address many of the issues, but not all. It will take several years for the tools and vendors to evolve, and knowledge of the security risks must be factored into the cost-benefit discussion of virtualization. Because of the rush to adopt virtualization for server consolidation efforts, many of the issues are overlooked, best practices are not applied or, in some cases, the tools and technologies for addressing the security issues with virtualization are immature or nonexistent. As a result, through year 2009, 60% of production VMs will be less secure than their physical counterparts. Virtualization is not simply a set of technologies buried in infrastructure. It also has important ramifications on the business use of IT, and on business itself. IT customers are often reticent about sharing equipment with other business units, and losing control of where "their" applications and "their" data reside. Ideally, customers should focus on service levels and results, not on physical location or IT methodologies. In reality, this cultural issue needs to be overcome, and can be

by building success stories. The result, however, is a relationship between the business and IT that becomes more service-oriented, giving IT more flexibility on how work gets done (or how work is sourced). The ability to deploy capacity and server images virtually increases the speed of deployment roughly by a factor of 30 times. When customers are familiar with a deployment time of two months, a sudden shift to two days might require fundamental changes to business processes.

Eleven: Value within Select Vertical Markets

SaaS and Cloud computing offer advantages many vertical markets. Implications and impact to the Federal Government, Energy, Aviation and Healthcare sectors are discussed.

FEDERAL GOVERNMENT

The Federal Government has identified the Internet as a national strategic asset. Cloud computing is a central part of this asset by providing strategic competitive advantage and enabling new capabilities. Given the fact that Cloud computing platforms will become an important part of advanced software systems, the United States has a vested interest in developing and maintaining a robust United States industry. Two public policy priorities which help the U.S. Federal Government maintain this competitive edge in Cloud computing are highlighted below.

Promote the free flow of secure data around the world
The Cloud computing business model works best when there is a free flow of secure information across borders. Currently, an entity or individual located in one country can have its data processed and stored in another country and enjoy secure, authenticated access to its information anywhere in the world.

Theoretically, an entity located in one country can have its data processed and stored in another country. In reality, there is no coherent international policy to govern how data should be retained or used. International rules and laws are confusing and inconsistent. Enterprises and governments overseas, whether justified or unjustified, have expressed reluctance to have their data stored and processed in the United States. Surveillance actions have raised concerns for these companies and countries about the United States as a safe location for international data. Existing security controls and privacy policies on the part of private entities will have to be modified to allay this concern. If these fears are allowed to fester, foreign enterprises could refuse to allow their data to be stored and processed in the United States, global data flows will be disrupted, United States competitiveness could be damaged, and the Cloud computing model would likely be undermined. Additionally, it is likely some countries will create their own cloud infrastructure and promote usage of national cloud products, thus adding to the cross border data flow issues in some ways, and subtracting from them in others.

The Federal Government could take the following actions to increase the global free flow of secure data to increase the strategic advantage of the United States:

- Establish a policy team to study potential harmonization of international rules on data use, storage and flow.

- Convey at the highest levels of the Administration that America's efforts to fight terror and crime will be matched by a deep respect for civil liberties and personal privacy. It is especially important to emphasize this message to foreign governments and in oversees business circles. The President, the Secretary of State, the Attorney General, and the Secretary of Commerce should incorporate this message into their public statements and share it privately with other world leaders.

- Hold private, bilateral discussions with foreign law enforcement agencies to emphasize the U.S. government's respect for personal privacy and its commitment to due process and the rule of law when

accessing information about foreign citizens that is
stored in the United States.

- Look into misuse of information residing in databases
  stored in the U.S. in our fight against terrorism and
  work on ways of preventing this misuse.

- Update U.S. government surveillance laws and ensure
  law enforcement investigations and intelligence-
  gathering activities involving data stored in the U.S. are
  done according to the rule of law.

Get Government on the Cloud

Many government agencies are overwhelmed by the sheer scope
and complexity of their IT operations and are spending increasing
proportions of their IT budget on operations, maintenance and
technology upgrades of their IT systems. Failed projects and
cost overruns are only the most obvious indicators. Numerous
government data breaches, the difficulty and expense of attracting
skilled IT professionals to the public sector, and stove-piped
information systems that prevent data-sharing across agencies are
testimony to the scope of the problem.

Cloud computing can help address many of the government
issues. Because Cloud computing applications are sold on a
renewable, per-user subscription or per-usage basis, payments are
spread out over time and there is much less risk of a costly failure.
Because Cloud computing applications reside on the Internet,
network or Wide Area Network (WAN), government customers
can use them where doing so offers additional or better value and
functionality than existing IT systems. Additionally, the cloud
provider regularly updates Cloud computing applications. The
government customers get the choice to maintain systems and
invest in hardware, data storage, software upgrade fees, cooling
and infrastructure costs, the choice to invest in the cloud, or the
choice to do both. Cloud computing applications are easy to use

and customize, therefore government customers can avoid getting locked into products that quickly become outdated. Combined, these benefits can create agility, flexibility, cost savings and better functionality for Federal agencies.

In order to accelerate the government's adoption of Cloud computing where appropriate, the Chief Technology Officer for the Federal Government should develop a Cloud computing framework. Key elements of such a plan should include the following:

- Require all Federal agencies to assess and report on which of their IT needs are best suited for or enhanced by Cloud computing.

- Assess how Cloud computing can provide more cost effective and elastic business continuity capabilities.

- Launch pilot Cloud computing projects across a range of government agencies and applications to better understand its benefits and limitations for diverse government needs.

- Leverage the collaboration tools that Cloud computing makes possible to solicit and receive feedback from American citizens to improve the functioning of democratic government.

- Clarify the government procurement process to allow information technology to be purchased as a subscription service.

- Direct the Federal CIO Council to work with the Federal CISO Council, which is being proposed as part of the Federal Information Security and Management Act (FISMA) reform, to identify and initiate security standardization activities related to the adoption of Cloud computing for the Federal government, including system security Certification and

Accreditation guidelines and mapping between industry security standards and NIST, defense, and other applicable security standards.

- Include Cloud computing as a complement to the Federal government's current Shared Services programs since both models are predicated on the need to drive down cost per-user while providing enhanced services.

Business, consumers, and entrepreneurs are rapidly adopting Cloud computing as a way to cut costs, improve productivity, and drive innovation. As Cloud computing is increasingly used as a global solution, its strategic importance will only grow. The Federal Government should make decisive action to leverage Cloud computing in order to enhance U.S. competitiveness and transform government operations.

ENERGY

There are several areas of the Energy market where SaaS appears to have taken a firm hold.

Energy Market Trading: OASIS (Open Access Same-Time Information System) is a web-based US energy market system formalized by the Federal Energy Regulatory Commission (FERC) and created to provide power marketers a mechanism to view power transmission and service availability. It is also the primary method by which high-voltage transmission lines are reserved for moving wholesale quantities of electricity. Once the transmission line is reserved, an electronic tag (e-Tag) must be submitted. An e-Tag is an electronic document of an energy transaction specifying the path, duration and timeframe of the transaction. For a more global perspective, the Intercontinental Exchange (ICE) is the largest exchange of energy commodities in the world, linked directly to individuals and firms looking to trade in oil, natural gas, jet-fuel, emissions, electric power and commodity derivatives. Due to the high level of web-based information sharing and increased exposure to web technologies, there is growing acceptance in this area for SaaS solutions.

Open Access Technology International (OATI) is an example of a company specializing in the energy market supporting SaaS and is the largest vendor of SaaS energy solutions. Their software products encompass all aspects of energy management; energy trading and risk management, transmission management, congestion management, NERC compliance, and smart grid development and management. They also handle over 96% of the e-tagging in the North American market. While OATI's products can be delivered on servers located within their customers' facilities, most choose to use OATI's dedicated SAS 70-certified hosting facility. They enjoy the inherent benefits of SaaS; limited or no hardware investment, reduced maintenance costs, quick implementation, and product upgrades that are not only nearly transparent but are also up to date with the ever changing compliance requirements and regulations of the energy markets.

Operations

There are several aspects of facility operations within the Oil and Gas industry that are supported by SaaS-based solutions. One is the fundamental operation of the facility or company and the traditional business and human resources support requirements. From a hardware and equipment perspective, remote computers installed within field systems can be used to monitor flow, level, and other performance indicators, sending their information to central stations for real-time analysis.

Avatar Systems is a company that provides IT products for the petroleum industry. They offer their Petroware 2000 oil and gas accounting environment both as a stand-alone locally hosted application and as a SaaS-delivered, subscription-based application. The SaaS delivery model option is meant to allow smaller companies access to the full-featured solution at a greatly reduced cost. Another application, RAPID, provides similar features but is designed specifically for implementation under the SaaS delivery model. Both applications feature support for expenditure authorization, joint interest billing, accounts payable, payroll, accounts receivable, revenue distribution, depreciation, depletion, and amortization, and general ledger.

Implicit Monitoring Solutions is a leading provider of remote asset performance and control monitoring services for the oil and gas industry. Their application, Intellisite, includes monitoring products for electronic flow metering monitoring, rotating equipment (compressors, pumps, generators) monitoring, tank level monitoring, pump off control monitoring, cathodic protection monitoring, and GPS asset location tracking and monitoring. Remote terminal units or other suitable communications devices are co-located with the devices being monitored. Critical field production data is collected and converted into a web-based format to help operators and producers efficiently and economically manage their fields, well sites, and pipelines. The "total field view" enables producers to improve the performance of well sites, send out alarms to avert a costly shutdown, avoid the escalating investment in technology, and help meet regulatory and compliance standards. As with most of the other companies, there are several ways for a customer to take advantage of this product. They can subscribe to the full-featured SaaS solution, with data being collected and formatted at the Implicit data center and made available via the Internet, or they can collect their own data and use the Intellisite application for formatting and reporting.

Regulatory Compliance

It is probably safe to say that most energy producers collect, organize and report on significant quantities of data for the purpose of confirming regulatory compliance. SaaS and the Internet have enabled the real time management of the various aspects of compliance, including water, air, waste, safety and health. San Diego Gas and Electric (SDG&E) is using a SaaS-based compliance management solution from Enviance. Their

Palomar Energy Center is the first new gas-fired energy plant to be built in San Diego in more than 30 years. Complex compliance requirements drove SDG&E to seek a robust solution that included on-demand Internet access, flexible reporting, seamless upgrades, self-administration with permissions and rights for users, and integration with a data historian. The implementation and training of the selected Enviance application was completed in less than four months. The facility uses Enviance daily to track tasks and incidents, as well as to generate reports and conduct audits in the areas of Air, Water, Waste, Land planning and natural resources, transportation licenses, safety, training, and energy-related requirements for the California Energy Commission, U.S. Department of Energy and the California Public Utilities Commission.

Crisis Management

Although not specifically advertised as a SaaS-delivered application, there is one web-based tool that was very interesting and worth mentioning. BP recently implemented a Crisis Management System using 3D satellite imagery, real-time weather data, and a visual representation of company's workers, their homes, and corporate assets. The web-based tool allows the BP Crisis Team, management, and executives from around the world to see the same information in real time. Using the Gulf as an example, BP has about 2000 people on platforms. When a hurricane comes through the company needs to decide who and what needs to be moved in the Gulf and the low-lying coastal areas. After Hurricanes Katrina and Rita hit in year 2005, BP realized they needed a faster and more automated way to collect and analyze information, monitor updates, and make informed decisions. Their Crisis Management System eventually became primarily a fusion of Microsoft's Virtual Earth and weather information (storm/hurricane paths, probability zones, and infrared satellite imagery) from ImpactWeather, Inc. The system can monitor many different climate events and their potential impact to BP resources, including earthquakes, wildfires, and ice storms. Further improvements to the system are planned, adding supply chain management, VOIP, text messaging and other mobile communications. A goal is to be able to allow employees in affected areas to call in via their phone or the Internet to let the company know where they are, their condition, and if any assistance is required. It appears that the energy market has embraced the technology that makes SaaS possible and is using SaaS in creative and productive ways. Web-based and SaaS applications were associated with most of the major energy companies that were researched. Most providers provide at least two options for their products: fully hosted SaaS delivery or their application resident on the customers' servers. Several providers I researched marketed their own applications and SaaS infrastructure, but also solicited other software vendors to provide their software as well, for a fee.

AVIATION

In order to have a competitive advantage in the Aviation market today, companies have to maximize air traffic throughput while reducing overall costs and turnaround time. Companies also have to ensure that they are compliant, safe and reliable. SaaS allows companies to focus on their core competencies by managing the non-core aspects of the business more efficiently through improved processes. SaaS can be used to manage resources, capacity, forecasting, and scheduling. Implementing SaaS in these areas will reduce turnaround time as well as increase the availability of resources and materials. SaaS can also help increase air traffic throughput by improving communications with customers and suppliers through use of web application services and/or share-point services. SaaS should also be considered for risk management, document management and storage, configuration management, and compliance management. SaaS principles could also be applied to the core of avionics as well by providing updates to software or computer programs for its weapons systems, as well as bug fixes and patches. It could also be used to update all Global Positioning Systems (GPS). Another area where SaaS is beneficial to the aviation market, both commercial and government, is in production and procurement. Within the government, product development and sustainment goes in cycles. We have reached the end of the research and development cycle and we have moved into life cycle sustainment and modernization. Many of the defense electronics that were developed in the late 1990's are being built and deployed now. Applying SaaS principles to production and procurement allows for faster deployments at decreased costs to the customer. As defense budgets decline and the cost to build new platforms (aircraft, ships, and/or vehicles) increase, the emphasis is on upgrading or modernizing existing systems in order to extend the life of the platform. Also the amount of time to activate and integrate has shortened from years to months. The Air Force is using SaaS for its on-demand supply chain management solutions. SaaS principles have allowed the Air Force to improve weapons systems availability while reducing parts inventory within the service supply chain. By streamlining their processes, they have been working towards combining hundreds of programs into one integrated logistics solution. Over the last several years there has been a significant shift in demand from hard-core development efforts to more commercial off the shelf (COTS) type products. Customers are interested in a plug and play environment where the products can be easily changed out and can be integrated with other systems easily. This is not just the case in the United States. It is also the case overseas. As more and more of our military assets are being purchased internationally, this plug and play environment is gaining importance. Countries such as Spain, Japan, and Korea are purchasing our technology and learning how to replicate that technology within their own countries. Therefore, in order to compete in international markets it will be important to offer products (cafeteria style) that will plug in and play with other vendor's equipment.

HEALTHCARE

The Healthcare industry requires a premium level of data management, communication and collaboration. Therefore analyzing the way a healthcare facility accesses this vital information requires more than just a review of the bottom line. Some of the most common criteria that hospitals/medical facility are considering when looking at leveraging SaaS are:

- Security and HIPAA compliance and control
- Readability of scanned images – even on EKG and pulmonary function tests
- Ability to catalog like they are set up not fitting a vendor format
- Easy access – ability to view all of a patient's activities then select what is wanted
- Intuitive software requiring no learning curve
- Control of who is allowed access
- 24-hour access with chart retrieval while records are being scanned
- Paper storage as a safety net
- Speed in converting – ability to scan quickly and upload to SaaS

Although every facility has their own requirements, these are just some of the more common ones. A variety of companies — from private health-care providers and insurance companies to big technology firms such as Microsoft HealthVault and Google Health — are developing and launching sites, most of them free, which allow patients to keep personal health records. Patients can input their records themselves or have them added by the few doctor's offices and other medical facilities that keep compatible electronic records online. Because the field is so new, standards and legislation are under development. And privacy advocates worry about sensitive records falling into the wrong hands. However, nearly everyone applauds the idea behind the records: it aims to bring the notoriously slow-to-computerize health records out of the era of manila folders and scribbled notes and into the future of electronic information that can be transported with the click of a button. In healthcare, an industry plagued by high cost and inefficiencies, the government is playing a large role in the adoption of SaaS. The government provides to 46% of the national healthcare expenses in the US and is looking for ways to ensure healthcare providers document work in a more efficient manner. SaaS vendors are concentrating on practice management that will enable healthcare providers to control inefficiencies and related high costs. Companies like IBM are currently working on a solution to do on-demand information management. Also, smaller vendors are focusing on practice management, such as digital medical records and imaging, so doctors can run their practice more efficiently. In addition, pharmaceutical companies are looking to leverage technology to reduce overall spending and increase their margins. There are some research and development initiatives that are currently in progress related to the healthcare market and how SaaS and a managed service model can be leveraged. Currently, the pharmaceutical industry is looking to potentially move their manufacturing locations to an offshore location in order to reduce their overall costs. The tracking and chain-of-custody of those pharmaceuticals becomes that much more important. In addition, companies like GSK are shipping 80% of their shipments via air, which is an expensive mode of transportation for retail shipments. In addition, they ship some temperature sensitive freight, which is critical that it is not delayed to the market. Some of the solutions that can assist in meeting these challenges include review of the entire inventory profile to determine what can go via surface re-plan routes based on mode shift, report chain of custody upon query and instantly report spoilage or tampering of items—which frequently occurs at the ports. The customer would be able to view this information via a SaaS model over the Internet and receive real time information about the shipments leveraging a managed service cost model. The value add is that they could potentially experience significant cost reduction in freight spent for target items, maintain service levels to their customers, reduce inventory spoilage, and loss and potentially reduce the number of shipments which would in turn reduce the administrative labor incurred per unit shipped. According to an article by AMI-Partners "Software-as-Service Hot Spots: Construction, Healthcare, and Financial", there are over 500 SaaS vendors in the U.S. alone. The report states that these SaaS vendors are beginning to offer services that match the requirements of the vertical industries. Vendors in the healthcare services markets are working to improve communication within the company and a company's collaboration with business partners today. It is recommended that companies become familiar with the SaaS vendors and their capabilities to better understand how we can provide a total solution for our government and commercial partners within the healthcare market. Research is being conducted today by many companies, and in order for them to become, and stay, competitive within this market; additional investment in research and development projects is necessary. Additionally understanding the customer's requirements would help in the development of more cost effective solutions.

Twelve: What Should My Business Enterprise Do Now?

Five discontinuities will combine to overwhelm the traditional practices of advanced software development organizations: Web 2.0, Software as a Service, global-class computing, the consumer orientation of IT and open source software. Advanced software development managers who are in charge of workplace applications need to rethink the fundamental principles that have guided the organization over the past few decades; for example, in providing a secure, controlled advanced software environment that serves all an enterprise's needs. Advanced software development organizations need to experiment with free-form environments to take advantage of the value generated by communities. They need to help selected users innovate. They need to stop taking responsibility for supporting and managing all workplace tools. And they need to adapt their approach so as to segment users according to their role and the value they produce.

Five major trends will force the IT organization to change the way it supports workers. The intensity of these trends will grow through at least year 2011.

1. Web 2.0 centers around social interaction and social networks — the valuable information that can be harvested from them, the personal relationships that can be developed through them, and the business processes that can become more effective because of social process facilitation.

2. SaaS provides new application capabilities on scalable platforms, a flexible alternative to packaged applications or those developed in-house.

3. Global-class applications do not force users to run a specific, application provider's system image. Examples such as eBay auctions, Amazon e-tailing and Yahoo search have already generated new business models (and new industries). Global-class systems include massive distributed systems, each of which might control millions of CPUs and related data stores. Global-class systems redefine how computing is done and will rewrite the substance and structure of many industries.

4. Consumer IT continues to make its way into the enterprise as workers turn to the devices and applications they use at home for functions that the IT organization does not provide.

5. Open-source software will exacerbate each of the four trends above.

These emerging discontinuities reinforce each other, and their combined effect will prove far stronger than the individual trends. IT managers who oversee workplace applications need to incorporate these trends into their long-term planning.

Four actions, discussed in detail below, can help IT managers take advantage of, rather than just react to, these five trends:

- Experiment with free-form environments
- Help users innovate
- Stop trying to provide everything
- Segment users
- Pay attention to Privacy and Confidentiality issues

EXPERIMENT WITH FREE-FORM ENVIRONMENTS

The community activities at the center of Web 2.0 technology represent emergent reality. No one preordained the forms, structures and processes of the Web. Rather, these emerged unforeseen from the hundreds of millions of users and billions of interactions that shape the social context of the Web. Just as free markets set prices, the invisible hand of the marketplace determines what people do and find valuable on the Web. "Folksonomies," "tag clouds" and the like provide the mechanism for turning individual actions into collective knowledge. That same invisible hand also dictates which new technologies and business models will win and which will lose — and the situation can change overnight, with new winners emerging and old winners disappearing at the will of the market. This environment runs contrary to the instincts of detail-oriented IT managers who are used to engineered systems. They often want to wall off the enterprise from an environment that is disorganized, unmethodical, wasteful and inconsistent, and where people and relationships take precedence over formal procedures and policies. Companies must not ignore the value that continually emerges from the Web, despite the tumultuous way "the best solutions" morph overnight. They too need to provide free-form, open environments to facilitate productive social interactions and to allow patterns of behavior, interaction with the rest of the business ecosystem and new business models (and opportunities) to emerge and evolve over time.

HELP USERS INNOVATE

Innovation speeds economic development. Apply this general rule to your enterprise by helping selected users interact in an open environment and thereby innovate. Allow them to exploit Web-based tools and share their experiences with other users:

- Start with informal project management tools.

- Experiment with free-form, searchable "personal Web pages"

- Encourage social discourse and allied publish-and-subscribe models (such as wikis, blogs, Really Simple Syndication [RSS] and Atom feeds).

- Test folksonomies, tag clouds and mash ups that collect and display users' sense of what is valuable in the system. Users can then navigate by keying on tags or types of user.

- Harden your systems (100% content inspection and strong authentication are two key approaches) to limit liabilities created by loosening some controls on users.

- Above all, let some users fail. Failure can breed success.

STOP TRYING TO PROVIDE EVERYTHING

For the IT organization, the greatest consequence of the five trends may be that they will give business units (and selected users) more independence to set their own IT direction. In addition, business models, marketing and distribution will shift radically. As a result, companies will embrace some powerful new ways of using IT to implement their business strategy. In fact, rogue users and departments are already starting to do this today. Their spending on the hundreds or thousands of available software services and other new tools fall below the IT organization's radar; and low-cost, readily available open-source software contributes to the success of SaaS. In many cases users can get their project done before they could have filed a formal proposal with their own IT organization. And they can do it seemingly at a fraction of the cost of a centrally provided "solution." IT organizations lack the operating models necessary to deliver these types of situational, ad hoc, often collaborative applications at a moment's notice. This is not a malignant trend. By applying some wisdom and exploiting the wisdom of the (rapidly emerging) Web 2.0 marketplace, companies can reap significant benefits outside the traditional bounds of the enterprise IT environment. For example, Procter & Gamble replaced traditional focus groups with Web-based tools to support (and glean valuable market information from) communities of consumers. It also used Internet-based markets to engage outside researchers to help it innovate and grow more rapidly. First, the IT organization should admit that it can no longer compete with the Web in providing many personal and social tools, nor should it. Instead, the IT organization should define what it is really good at (for instance, large-scale, long-term enterprise-wide projects) and, for the other activities, play the role of advisor and facilitator. For example, the IT organization may provide advice about procurement, but will leave the actual purchase (or rental, as in SaaS) of a wiki up to the business unit. Note: enterprise-scale IT may not be good enough anymore. Some companies will exploit global class architectures provided by vendors such as Google and Microsoft to create new IT procurement models, even new business models. Global-class computing will challenge many assumptions for how to construct, deploy and manage content-related, communication, collaboration and social networking technologies. More commonly, companies will enable or encourage large portions of their workers to provide their own computing resources. By year 2010, more than half of all employees entering the workforce will choose "guest networks" for performing their jobs (0.7 probability). Finally, the enterprise or IT organization can no longer assume responsibility for supporting and managing all IT systems that workers use. If the IT organization allows some users to experiment with new Web-based software and communities, or even to provide their own computers, those users must take personal responsibility for doing.

For these experiments, the IT organization should:

- Select users who are likely to behave responsibly

- Explain to users the risks of using new technologies and approaches

- Set guidelines for use to minimize the risks of compliance problems

- Define what support the IT organization will provide and how it will give this support

- Outline the costs and responsibilities that the users will have to bear

SEGMENT USERS ACCORDING TO THEIR ROLE AND THE VALUE THEY PRODUCE

The IT organization should stop providing the same support to everyone. Many do so because a uniform approach makes the IT environment easier to manage (for example, everyone gets the same model computer with the same operating system. IT managers should segment users, including all those in the business ecosystem, such as people from partners, suppliers and customers. Some groups of users will benefit by having new or extra functions delivered via SaaS. Social networking technologies will allow self-organizing groups of users to produce more. In these situations, the IT organization needs to play the role of facilitator, helping users who want to experiment with social software, but not making all the choices. During this experimental phase, people would not be forced to use an implementation of a wiki or some other tool, nor would all people have to use the wiki for it to succeed.

PAY ATTENTION TO PRIVACY AND CONFIDENTIALITY ISSUES

Standardization of terminology and terms of service would help users understand the risks and consequences of using a cloud provider. At present, however, the best a user can do is to select a cloud provider carefully based on its terms of service and privacy policy. Reading and understanding the terms of service may be the single most important thing for an individual to do before using a cloud provider. Regrettably, the terms of service are often complex, and may require a high level of interest and persistence to thoroughly parse and understand. An alternative is to avoid cloud providers altogether until better protections for users are available. A business or agency should be fully aware of any privacy or other obligations that attach to data being shared with a cloud provider.

CONCLUSION: SAAS AND THE AGILE BUSINESS ENTERPRISE

The business climate continues to get tougher, more competitive, more challenging and more prone to change. Adapting to change poses a major impediment to achieving market leadership and competitive differentiation, as well as to ensuring survival. The emergence of an "always on" connected world has brought about a collapse of distance and time as the speed of information exchange has increased worldwide. This collapse is evidenced by the widespread reduction in product life cycles, the reduction in the duration of sustainable differentiation, the increase in competition and the blurring of business boundaries across all industries. The greater information exchange also increases the knowledge, expectations and choices of buyers, thereby tipping the traditional balance of power. The increased power of buyers has forced changes in the cost and pricing models of manufacturers' products. Manufacturers or service providers that formerly passed their costs on to buyers are now forced to lower their production or provision costs to make their products and services attractive to buyers. Buying power is reducing the overall profitability of industries. As a result of these and other forces, lower profits and rapid change are structural realities for business, exposing weaknesses in every part of the organization: policy, strategy, operations, relationships and infrastructure. Changes in the business environment are outpacing the time it takes an organization to respond. An enterprise that cannot effectively reduce the time required responding to change invites competitors to grab market share, supersede its position and even imperil its survival in the market. All these factors have narrowed the window of opportunity for businesses and are demanding new rules for recognizing opportunities and reacting effectively.

Organizations need new ways to identify change and to respond quickly. They are being drawn to a new goal for agility: the ability of an organization to sense environmental change and respond efficiently and effectively to that change. To navigate effectively through the dynamic market conditions that have given rise to the new focus on agility, organizations often must make major business transformations, change business direction, re-engineer business processes, and accelerate performance and execution. They will have this transformation readily enabled through the leveraged use of SaaS and Cloud computing technology that their enterprise architectures and IT infrastructures support. An organization's agile performance must be proactively managed from a single, unifying, overarching business architecture that optimizes SaaS and Cloud computing investments, leverages the organization's main sources of competitive advantage, and supports dynamically changing organizational goals and priorities. Best practices often provide great value to an enterprise. With agility, the same will be seen. However, no set of best practices for agility likely will be applied consistently from enterprise to enterprise or from year to year. The reason is that agility means different things to different people, and the factors that contribute to agility can vary, depending on the situation. SaaS and Cloud computing technology facilitates and enables agility in the organization. Each organization will also have a different set of business challenges and a unique architectural footprint that will require different SaaS and Cloud computing deployment strategies to support and enhance agility.

A common belief is that, to improve their agility, enterprises must focus on the new technology of SaaS and Cloud computing. This is not true. The ability to be agile involves optimized use of new technologies, like SaaS and Cloud computing, along with established technologies. Stronger effectiveness in SaaS and Cloud computing improves an enterprise's ability to be agile because it potentially means that fewer people, less money and less time must be allocated to solve a particular problem.

The ideal architecture will include the appropriate and unique mix of technologies and organizational best practices to:

- Enable an organization to be aware of the changing business environment
- Be flexible enough to handle a wide range of alternative conditions and actions
- Be efficient and effective in producing results

SaaS and Cloud computing-enabled agility is an emerging management discipline. Although heavily powered by technology, agility is ultimately a human-centric effort and must be introduced with care and sophisticated change management. The drivers that created a demand for agility are not going away; they are only going to worsen. Sensing environmental change and responding efficiently and effectively to that change are not new goals. Transforming the act from a chaotic and haphazard effort into a SaaS and Cloud computing enabled management discipline is the focus of an agility strategy. Successful and leading enterprises will recognize and treat SaaS and Cloud computing-enabled agility as an emerging management discipline. They will understand the tools and techniques of agility, and they will be prepared to teach and institute agility best practices as they emerge. Managers will be trained on agility concepts, and they will review their wins and losses as they attempt to be agile. As with all management disciplines, learning comes from doing, and doing sometimes means failing. Although agility will emerge as a management discipline, it will not be a universal discipline practiced in the same way by each enterprise. Agility and innovation are close partners. Enterprises should expect to leverage best practices from their peers and industries, but they also should remember that agility is an effort that works best when customized to the enterprise's specific capabilities and needs. Variations in SaaS and Cloud computing inflection point strategies do and should exist. It is the role of executives in each company to recognize what mix of these advanced software strategies/imperatives makes sense, given the unique set of challenges and resources at each organization. Executives who lead today will win tomorrow by defining their own SaaS and Cloud computing inflection point strategy.

ACKNOWLEDGEMENTS

The Software as a Service Inflection Point grew from a number of independent research activities that came together at just the right time.

As the Principle Investigator of the independent research and development project "Thunderhead" focused on investigating of Cloud computing and demonstration of the use of public / private cloud capabilities, I became aware of the architectural options, business and technical challenges and potential business opportunities that SaaS and Cloud computing offer. From a practitioners perspective I, along with my team, developed a demonstration that highlighted these elements and provided a deep understanding of how to position this advanced software capability, and develop a thoughtful and insightful book. It is through this independent research initiative that I came to understand that SaaS and Cloud Computing had indeed reached an inflection point as it relates to adoption.

I'm a member of the Information Technology Association of America, Public Sector Cloud Computing Committee. In early January 2009, just before the inauguration of Barrack Obama as President, this team was charged with providing input to the new administration on the impact and uses of Cloud computing in Government. I enjoyed working with this cross industry team in developing a position paper that details what Cloud computing is, how the Government can leverage it, and the benefits to citizens that can be derived. Providing input is the first step, and I continue to collaborate with this team and other industry / government advisory organizations in ensuring that we can fully apply and benefit from the agility and cost savings this advanced software model provides.

Acknowledgements

As Executive Champion of the Lockheed Martin Executive Development and Growth Enhancement Software as a Service Project, I led a team of eight high potentials in the development of a detailed brief on SaaS and Cloud computing that was delivered to the company president and her direct reports. This team was highly motivated and helped to shape my thoughts around the implementation of SaaS, as a consumer and provider. I learned to develop an easy to understand logic around the topic and developed much of the Reading Guide of my interactions with this team. I continue to work with them in development of a near deployable SaaS / Cloud solutions utilizing application platform as a Service to build custom applications and access them from a handheld edge device like an iPhone.

I truly want to thank my wife for her caring and support. As an author herself she has a unique understanding of what is required to organize, write, edit and publish a book. The Software as a Service Inflection Point would not exist without her.

LIST OF ACRONYMS

AMI	Amazon Machine Images
API	Application Programmable Interface
B2B	Business to Business
BPEL4WS	Business Process Execution Language for Web Services
COM/DCOM	Competent Object Model/Distributed Competent Object Model
CORBA	Common Object Request Broker Architecture
COTS	Commercial off The Shelf
CRM	Customer Resource Management
DCE	Distributed Computing Environment
DMZ	Dematerialized Zone
DSig	Digital Signature
EAI	Enterprise Application Integration
EC2	Elastic Cloud Compute
EDI	Electronic Data Inter-exchange
ERP	Enterprise Resource Planning
ESB	Enterprise Service Bus
FERC	Federal Energy Regulatory Commission
FISMA	Federal Information Security and Management Act
GPS	Global Positioning System
HTTP	Hypertext Transfer Protocol
ICE	Intercontinental Exchange
I/O	Input/Output
IT	Information Technology
J2EE	Java 2 Enterprise Edition
M&A	Merger and Acquisition
O&M	Operations and Maintenance
OASIS	Organization for the Advancement of Structured Information Standards

OATI	Open Access Technology International
OMG	Object Management Group
OS	Operating System
REST	Representational State Transfer
ROI	Return on Investment
RSS	Really Simple Syndication
SAML	Security Assertion Markup Language
SDG&E	San Diego Gas and Electric
SEAP	Saas-enabled Application Platform
SI	System Integrator
SLA	Service Level Agreement
SMTP	Simple Mail Transfer Protocol
SOA	Service Oriented Architecture
SOAP	Simple Object Access Protocol
SQS	Simple Queue Service
TCO	Total Cost of Ownership
TCP/IP	Transmission Control Protocol/Internet Protocol
UDDI	Universal Description, Discovery and Integration
UI	User Interface
VM	Virtual Machine
VP	Vice-President
W3C	World Wide Web Consortium
WAN	Wide Area Network
WSDL	Web Services Definition Language
WS-I	Web Services Interoperability Organization
XML	Extensible Markup Language
XSLT	Extensible Stylesheet Language Transformations

Reading Group Guide: Questions and Topics for Discussion

SaaS and Cloud computing has become the latest in a series of popular industry terms and, as such, is used in many contradictory ways. Underneath the fog, there are trends — such as global-class architecture, Web platforms, massively scalable processing and the Internet — that are converging to fuel the Cloud computing phenomenon. The platform angle, in particular, will enable composite applications and composite businesses, and has the potential to have a profound impact on IT and business. Organizations must evolve to deal with the changes, and understand what hype is safe to ignore. Cloud computing is an alternate delivery and acquisition model for IT-related services. This phenomenon will shift the way purchasers of IT products and services contract with vendors, and the way those vendors deliver their wares. This leads to comparisons with the Industrial Revolution and the resulting impact on the way many organizations approach the delivery of business services enabled by IT. Cloud computing heralds an evolution of business — no less influential than the era of e-business — in positive and negative ways. It has been used in many contradictory ways. Overall, there are definite trends toward cloud platforms and massively scalable processing. Virtualization, service orientation and the Internet have converged to sponsor a phenomenon that enables individuals and businesses to choose how they will acquire or deliver IT services, with reduced emphasis on the constraints of traditional software and hardware licensing models. Many other things are different as well, including risk profiles, amounts of outsourcing and payment plans. Companies will get to choose between buying the servers and running applications in-house, buying the IT infrastructure as a service and running their tailored portfolios on that, buying the IT infrastructure and

SaaS, or buying varying degrees of IT-enabled BPO. All this will allow economies of scale that can reduce prices. Services delivered through the "cloud" will foster an economy based on delivery and consumption of everything from storage to computation to video to finance deduction management. SaaS and Cloud computing exposes potential risks and opportunities, and enables the next evolution of business.

How will Cloud computing be defined, and how will it evolve?

During the past 15 years, a continuing trend toward IT industrialization has grown in popularity. IT services delivered via hardware, software and people are becoming repeatable and usable by a wide range of customers and service providers. This is due, in part, to the commoditization and standardization of technologies, virtualization and the rise of service-oriented software architectures, and (most importantly) the dramatic growth in popularity/use of the Internet and the Web. Taken together, they constitute the basis of a discontinuity that amounts to a new opportunity to shape the relationship between those who *use* IT services and those who *sell* them. The discontinuity implies that the ability to deliver specialized services in IT can be paired with the ability to deliver those services in an industrialized and pervasive way. The reality of this implication is that users of IT-related services can focus on *what* the services provide them, rather than *how* the services are implemented or hosted.

How will Cloud computing affect the strategy and direction of IT and business?

The types of IT services that can be provided through a cloud are far-reaching. Compute facilities (such as Amazon Elastic Compute Cloud [Amazon EC2]) provide computational services so that users can use CPU cycles without buying computers. Storage services (such as Amazon Simple Storage Service [Amazon S3]) provide a way to store data and documents without having to continually grow farms of storage networks and servers. SaaS companies, such as salesforce.com, offer CRM services through their multi-tenant shared facilities so clients can manage their customers *without* buying software; more recently, they have offered platform services as well. This represents only the beginning of options for delivering all kinds of complex capabilities to businesses and individuals. The focus has moved up from the infrastructure implementations and onto the services that allow for access to the capabilities provided. Although many companies will argue about how the cloud services are implemented, the ultimate arbiter of success will be how the services are consumed and whether that leads to new business opportunities. The implementation can affect that outcome, but it represents only part of the overall value proposition.

CAN BUSINESS AGILITY BE ENHANCED BY SAAS AND CLOUD COMPUTING?

Business Agility is an organization's ability to respond to change. If the organization cannot respond well to change, it can lose competitive advantage or even cease to exist. In a world where change is becoming more rapid and less predictable, increased agility is obviously critical to corporate survival. Change also often presents important new opportunities. The focus on business agility is a primary driver for the rapid response and flexibility associated with the software delivery models associated with Cloud computing and SaaS, and the main reason we have reached an inflection point with regards to their adoption. Are there other significant drivers for SaaS and how can they be identified and measured? What business issues impacting agility could have a negative impact on SaaS adoption?

WHAT VENDORS, MARKETS AND INDUSTRIES WILL BE TRANSFORMED BY THE CLOUD COMPUTING PHENOMENON?

With any issue that has such high visibility as Cloud computing, there is significant potential to change the status quo in the IT market. As for IT vendors, the impact could be huge. Established vendors have great presence in traditional software markets. As new Web 2.0 and cloud business models evolve and become the province of not just consumer markets, a lot could change. The vendors are at widely different levels of maturity. The consumer-focused vendors are the most mature in delivering what Gartner calls a "cloud/Web platform" from technology and community perspectives; most investment in recent years has occurred in consumer services. The business-focused vendors have rich business services and, at times, are very mature at selling business services (for example, ADP). These vendors however have a narrow cloud/Web platform or do not necessarily provide a cloud/Web platform today. These are all potential vendors. Many vendors from different perspectives (traditional IT vendors, Web-centric vendors or vendors from other business, such as FedEx and ADP) were not technology providers but will play an important role in the overall cloud/Web platform market.

WHEN, WHERE, HOW AND WHY SHOULD COMPANIES EXPLOIT OFF-PREMISES, CLOUD COMPUTING SERVICES?

Cloud computing is an alternate delivery and acquisition model for IT-related services. This phenomenon will shift the way purchasers of IT products and services contract with vendors, and the way those vendors deliver their wares. This leads to comparisons with the Industrial Revolution and the resulting impact on the way many organizations approach the delivery of business services enabled by IT. Research in this area will focus on the potential advantages, as well as the risks and disadvantages, of exploiting external Cloud computing services. Discussion topics should include:

- Understanding and mitigating the risks associated with Cloud computing
- Determining which enterprise applications are good candidates for deployment using SaaS and Cloud Computing
- Analyzing the use of Internet technologies as a fundamental aspect of Cloud computing, and the degree to which this may limit the use of SaaS

WHICH NEW APPLICATIONS AND SOLUTIONS ARE NOW FEASIBLE DUE TO THE AVAILABILITY OF GLOBAL-SCALE, CLOUD COMPUTING SERVICES?

Using massive and distributed computing resources, global-class design principles, and new data models and Web-centric architectures and languages, providers of Cloud computing services can potentially offer platforms for building and delivering new applications. Given the economics of the cloud platform and the new business models emerging around the delivery of cloud-based services, these new applications could be created and delivered at a radically lower cost when compared with conventional approaches. However, Cloud computing is in its early stages, and the technological and business models are, as yet, unproven. Gartner's research in this area will examine the various architectures and business models to determine where they offer real opportunity, today and tomorrow.

WHICH MODELS, ARCHITECTURES, TECHNOLOGIES AND BEST PRACTICES SHOULD ENTERPRISES ADOPT FROM CLOUD

COMPUTING TO THEIR INTERNAL IT ENVIRONMENTS?

Off-premises computing resources are not new. What sets Cloud computing apart from traditional outsourcing and hosting approaches is providers' use of particular design models, architectures, technologies, and best practices to instantiate and support the delivery of an elastically scalable, service-oriented environment serving multiple constituents. The Cloud computing service provider has assembled and integrated elements in a unique way, and has often created custom hardware, software and/or processes to deliver the service. Enterprise IT users have long-desired a more agile, flexible and service-based environment for the delivery of internal applications or services, and Gartner has followed this trend as "real-time infrastructure." As Cloud computing gains momentum, and as particular approaches are shown to provide lower cost and greater flexibility, there is the potential to apply what has been learned to internal systems. In addition, most enterprises will be faced with managing an IT environment that will include cloud-based and internal resources. Research in this area will focus on what can and cannot be applied from the world of public Cloud computing services to create captive internal clouds. It will also examine how companies can create a symbiotic approach that combines the best of internal and external cloud services.

WHEN CAN A BUSINESS OR INDIVIDUAL SHARE PRIVATE INFORMATION WITH A CLOUD PROVIDER?

The United States has several privacy laws applicable to particular types of records or businesses. Some of these laws establish privacy standards that have bearing on a decision by a business to use a cloud provider. Others laws do not. Some laws specifically allow a business to share personal information with another company that provides support services to the business. Specific statutory references to the use of a service provider have no apparent pattern in privacy laws. Some privacy laws have them; some do not. For example, the Gramm-Leach-Bliley Act[16] restricts financial institutions from disclosing a consumer's personal financial information to a non-affiliated third party. Disclosure to a service provider is generally not restricted. However, the terms under which information is disclosed and the rights acquired by service providers could make a difference to the legality of the disclosure or subsequent use. Other laws, however, do limit the use of a cloud provider. What are the consequences of laws affecting decisions about using Cloud computing for business data? Both procedural and substantive barriers to the use of Cloud computing exist for some records and some businesses.

THE MARRIAGE OF BPM AND SOA

What's the best entry point to launch a service-oriented architecture implementation? Is it through business process management, an enterprise service bus or SOA governance?

Government Computer News
Published online: July 2008

I spoke recently with Mel Greer, a senior research engineer for the Advanced Technologies Office of Lockheed Martin, about this subject. Lockheed Martin's government clients are interested in all three approaches, but the one Greer thinks gives the most value is BPM. 'There is a value proposition associated with the marriage of SOA and business processes,' he said. SOA can be a key enabler for lining up technology with an organization's mission function, but it is only when SOA is linked up with business processes that an agency can reap tangible benefits from a process and flexibility perspective, Greer said. It is time to define some terms here. BPM, Greer said, is a discipline that provides the governance of a business process with the goal of improving the agility and operational performance of that process. The goal is not technical. SOA, on the other hand, is an application architecture approach, which is comprised of reusable components and services. In fact, enterprise architecture, BPM and SOA working in concert are the necessary ingredients required to ensure that there is a core alignment between an organization's business and IT strategies and more effective optimization of that IT environment, Greer said.

A Conversation with Melvin Greer

With the SOA adoption rate increasing fast, CIO Leadership Magazine talks to Melvin Greer, Director of the SOA Competency Center at Lockheed Martin, about his views on the uptake and considerations about the problems we might face.
Published online: Feb 2009

Q. What are the new and emerging trends you're seeing with respect to SOA?

A. There are a few great things happening with SOA. Firstly, we are clearly seeing increased focus on it; there's emphasis right across the board. As a company, Lockheed Martin is the largest provider of information technology to the U.S. government. However, its business moves beyond the 50 states to 50 countries worldwide. As a company we have a strong emphasis on SOA. However, you find that there's some good news and not so good news. The good news is that the idea of service-orientated architecture is having a significant impact on the approach people are taking to software development. That's a good thing because we are seeing a significant increase in the build of services and the use of services to build applications and the benefits associated with that are very much being realized. The second thing is that there are a number of standardization processes and efforts that are actually progressing. A number of Standards Organizations are spending a significant amount of time on SOA and are actually making quite good headway with respect to the development of standards that are guiding the capabilities. Thirdly, there are a number of tools which are now available that support an SOA-based approach to development activity. These tools allow us to take a business process and develop candidate services, evaluating the granularity of those services and move them into a transformational engine quickly. These kinds of tools are very much needed in order to continue with the idea of SOA. Lastly, there are a set of academic and industry researchers and partners, like Lockheed Martin, that are working on a wide range of relevant problems which is sure to increase and ease SOA adoption. Lockheed Martin is clearly one of the folks at the forefront of this activity and as the director of the SOA Competency Centre at Lockheed Martin I can assure you that not a day goes by when we don't work on developing solutions for hard problems of SOA.

The not so good news is that while we put significant effort in this area, things are evolving in many directions all at the same time; I guess the best way to characterize it is that they are evolving without a central compass. As such, success is achieved, albeit in a fragmented and muted way. Secondly, often we are framing our SOA discourse based on the vendors which are providing the tools to actually do the building of SOA-oriented solutions. Vendor partners are extremely important to us, but when the vendors are framing the SOA discourse, often that impedes our ability to have an open discussion without specific agendas. Thirdly, there seems to be a lack of agreement of a common theme of focus in SOA adoption and research activity, so in some cases you focus on the mission upon which this SOA activity is intended to support, and in the case of Lockheed Martin, these missions are things like command and control to the tactical edge, information dominance, and cyber security, or secure-cyber, but we also have other themes which are taking us away from the mission. These things are more concerned with the IT capability and this is not helping. Lastly, there is a danger that the SOA adoption and the research required to support it are actually being overlooked. At Lockheed Martin we spend a significant amount of money, millions a year, on research that is oriented around SOA and SOA approaches, however we are finding that there is more focus on the build activity and less associated to the research of hard problems.

Q. Why should companies take the leap towards SOA and what are the major benefits?

A. Companies like Lockheed Martin, and more specifically our customers, are under extreme pressures. The economic cycle in which we find ourselves today is exacerbating some of those pressures. However, there are really three main reasons why companies and agencies in the government should take this leap towards an approach which is orientated around services. Firstly, there is a significant increase in the frequency of change and this frequency, which used to take a year, is now taking less than a week. At the beginning of this fall we had a robust financial services market and a set of companies around that market. Today, those markets, and those companies, do not exist. Change is happening much faster. Secondly, the impact of that change is harder to respond to because previously the impact of change was easier to understand. One of the primary reasons companies want to move to an approach based around services is because they want to respond to the frequency and impact of this change. Organizations and enterprises want to become more agile and respond to market pressures, so they want to provide new, advanced capabilities which did not exist before and take advantage of these new approaches to enhance services to the citizens. The third reason is that the cost of maintaining legacy IT environments is continuing to rise. SOA is not the answer to every problem, but it certainly does allow for organizations and federal agencies to drive down the total cost of provisioning the types of capabilities they are really interested in providing services to.

Q. What are the opportunities for business transformation afforded by service oriented architecture and how can these opportunities help senior managers achieve their business goals?

A. There are a number of opportunities. Business transformation literally is afforded by service oriented architecture when we're able to take a look at total cost of ownership and cost reduction; this is the low-hanging fruit that most people are activity pursuing when they talk about the opportunities. Now, this is significant because just like the application of most technologies, there is an uptake in cost long before there is any cost reduction, and so this idea of cost reduction needs to be tempered with the realization that there is a need to constantly look at the longer-term, and enterprise strategy, when embarking down this path. The reason why people use service-oriented architecture is not because they want to implement new technologies that are hot off the shelf, but to respond to long term business pressures and change.

Another opportunity folks want to take advantage of is the idea of advanced capabilities. So when we think of advanced capabilities at Lockheed Martin we think about things like biometrics, advanced surveillance and intelligence, and we think about things like climatology and global ocean observing. These types of capabilities require a new way of looking at these problems. As such, the long-term approach that SOA provides and the establishment of these advanced capabilities is what we are very much interested in, in terms of opportunities to support our clients. Lastly, like most organizations, we are really interested in being able to expand into new and adjacent markets. For example, at Lockheed Martin we look at biometrics for areas of immigration to identify individuals. Moving forward, it would be good if we could use similar biometrics for ocean observing, and identify animals in a similar way. So this type of adjacent market penetration presents the kind of opportunities business executives are eager to take advantage of and SOA is a key enabler to help them do that.

Q. What are the main technologies involved in SOA engagements and what would you say are the key market drivers and inhibitors for SOA adoption?

A. There are a whole host of technologies and one of the roles we at the SOA Competency Centre at Lockheed Martin do is to try and filter through these technologies. The primary ones include the basic SOA fleet products which come from our vendor partners.

One of the things we like to highlight when we talk about technologies involved in SOA engagement is the contribution that SOA Governance provides with respect to the engagement. We have found that there are thousands of engagements that Lockheed Martin does with a high degree of competency. Managing services over their lifecycle is a key and strategic enabler to a successful SOA engagement. So SOA Governance cannot be overlooked. We are also very much using Open Source products in general and these products allow us to leverage a number of contributions across various development teams, but also contribute to those teams and help shape the capabilities that SOA technologies need in order to be successful. Moving forward, our focus will be on Cloud computing and SAAS technologies as well as Web 2.0 and social networking technologies. In terms of market drivers there is a significant amount of pressure on business and IT organizations to deliver applications which change rapidly and evolve as quickly as the business evolves. So business organizations are expecting the IT organization to provide a rapid response to change with optimal efficacy in motion, economy of effort, and energy in execution. So because of that, and other reasons, the IT organizations are investigating service oriented architecture as a key response to this kind of business expectation. In terms of inhibitors, I'd like to characterize them from an IT perspective. The reason for this is because when we take a look at the overall inhibitors to SOA adoption there are quire a few, but the ones which bubble to the surface relate to a series of technology disorders, and these technology disorders are having an impact on our ability to adapt SOA across an enterprise. I've identified four of the main inhibitors: the first I'm calling the Technology Alter-Syndrome. In this particular situation, an IT organization focuses on business first, and on the technology after, and then focuses all of its energy on the idea of technical purity around SOA, looking for a single truth around SOA for the enterprise. This is a major inhibitor because there is no single truth for SOA and in an enterprise, SOA can take many forms. The second inhibitor is the idea of Organizational and Financial Disorder. This is where the systems which are driving the organization are impairing it from enterprise thinking and enterprise development. This is a significant disorder because while the business leaders are in fact interested in moving SOA adoption forward, the organizational structure and particularly the financial reward systems, are inhibiting their ability to do so. This is manifest in the case of reuse of services and service ownership. Third is what I'm calling Not-Invested-Here-Dementia. This is part of a control phobia that impacts naming and reuse of services across the enterprise. This is to say, when organizations build services as part of a service orientated architecture construct, the naming and description associated with the services can serve as an inhibitor itself. So if we have a service named a particular name, which name itself could inhibit someone discovering the service and using it. Lastly, we have a hyper-sensitivity towards SOA Governance. When organizations want to deviate significantly from enterprise policy standards and methods, these kinds of things tend to be inhibitors to SOA adoption. As such, Lockheed Martin are trying to cure these inhibitors by increasing focus on SOA and creating a common language for an SOA approach. We are driving the metrics around SOA, and aim to create a stepwise solution.

Q. What is the measure for SOA Success and how much SOA is enough?

A. The measure of SOA success is in its ability to support business agility and respond to change. If SOA engagements are inhibiting businesses, organizations, or agencies, making them more rigid and susceptible to the impact of change; the less capable an organization is of achieving agility, then SOA is not implemented successfully. The idea of how much SOA is enough is a very good question. It is one of the things I would characterize as a hard problem. An SOA engagement should be big enough so that it demonstrates the various benefits described, and at the same time it needs to recognize that everything can't be SOA. This is one of the things I'd characterize as a hard problem that will constantly be looked at as we continue to move through this continuum of new technologies. When we talk about top of mind concerns of CIO's in the next twelve months, we will certainly see that SOA is acting as an on-ramp to other technologies. However, changing everything to SOA is probably not recommended any more than not doing any SOA. Having the right mix is what every organization will struggle to do.

Q. What is a SOA Hard Problem? How can these be overcome and what is their relation with Spiral Solution Development?

A. A SOA hard problem is comprised of three components. The first is that a hard problem will not go away over time. A hard problem is persistent. Second, a SOA hard problem left unresolved will have a significant negative impact on your SOA adoption plans for the enterprise. So some problems have minimal impact, some problems have a medium impact; a SOA hard problem is one that left unresolved will have a significantly negative impact. Thirdly, and probably most significant and important, is that resolving a SOA hard problem will require multiple disciplines, that come from inside and outside your own organization. A SOA hard problem is not one that a single enterprise can solve. It will require skills and intellectual capital that comes from collaboration between multiple different organizations. The nature of a hard problem requires unique techniques for solving, which we refer to as spiral solution development. A spiral is a technique which breaks down a hard problem with a series of smaller activities. At our Lockheed Martin SOA Competency Centre we identify a series of hard problems and break them into spirals that last between 30-90 days and each spiral produces an answer for a portion of the hard problem. There are two classes of problems: first engineering hard problems like dynamic discovery & composition. If we have 100's of services in the enterprise and no-one is able to find them and no-one is looking for them, then that's a problem- a very hard problem. As such, we need ways to encourage dynamic discovery of services. Second, design of services for context awareness is equally important so that the service will know at runtime the difference between 21 Blackjack and 21- the legal age for drinking. These kind of hard problems are important to try and solve if we are going to move SOA adoption forward. At Lockheed Martin we use spiral development to try and solve these problems.

Q. What do you foresee being of top of mind concerns for the CIO agenda in the next 12 months?

A. From an SOA perspective there are four things. We are going to see CIOs talk about a move from current SOA to an idea of web-oriented architecture, adding more scale and agility to the idea of SOA. Also, event-driven SOA, which will be engaged in a different design and programming model for software and in my opinion, will require a new breed of design and development tools. Thirdly, a new set of enterprise applications that will incorporate commercial technology to support real-time operational intelligence. In this particular case, the business will demand a more sophisticated and faster response to support these new business activities, so development patterns will need to shift towards event processing. Real-time information flow capabilities are also a key consideration but will require further investigation. Lastly, we will not be delivering whole final applications but instead we will build gadgets, allowing end-users to be responsible for their own final assembly of the application – adding so called 'mash-up' capability to their portfolio.

Melvin Greer is Senior Research Engineer, SOA Chief Architect, and Director SOA Competency Center, Lockheed Martin, Advanced Technologies Office. With over 20 years of systems and software engineering experience, he functions as a principal investigator in advanced research studies. He significantly advances the body of knowledge in basic research and critical, highly advanced engineering and scientific disciplines. Mr. Greer is a Strategist on the Information Technology Association of America, Cloud Computing Committee and membership in the Government Cloud Computing Community of Interest.

BIBLIOGRAPHY

(Endnotes)

1 http://microsoftpdc.com/View.aspx?post=http://
   channel9.msdn.com/posts/PDCNews/Windows-Azure-
   Announced/&tag

2 http://my.gartner.com/portal/server.pt?objID=219&open=5
   12&parentname=Gartner&mode=2&parentid=0&in_hi_us
   erid=1513914&PageID=466528&cached=false&space=Op
   ener

3 http://my.gartner.com/portal/server.pt?objID=219&open=5
   12&parentname=Gartner&mode=2&parentid=0&in_hi_us
   erid=1513914&PageID=466528&cached=false&space=Op
   ener

4 http://www.wiley.com/WileyCDA/WileyTitle/productCd-
   0471191752,descCd-authorInfo.html?print=true

5 http://microsoftpdc.com/View.aspx?post=http://
   channel9.msdn.com/posts/PDCNews/Windows-Azure-
   Announced/&tag=

6 http://www.microsoft.com/azure/whatisazure.mspx

7 .NET Service Bus White Paper

8 http://download.microsoft.com/download/e/4/3/e43bb484-
   3b52-4fa8-a9f9-ec60a32954bc/Azure_Services_Platform.
   pdf

9 http://code.google.com/appengine/docs/
   whatisgoogleappengine.html

10 http://www.ibm.com/developerworks/library/ar-cloudaws2/

Bibliography

11 http://www.ibm.com/developerworks/library/ar-cloudaws3/

12 http://www.ibm.com/developerworks/library/ar-cloudaws4/

13 http://aws.amazon.com/windows/

14 http://googleappengine.blogspot.com/2009/02/roadmap-update.html

16 http://www.govtrack.us/congress/bill.xpd?bill=s106-900&tab=summary

CPSIA information can be obtained at www.ICGtesting.com
Printed in the USA
BVOW060010270212

283776BV00001B/4/P